CONTEMPORARY

ISSUES
COMPANION

Race and Ethnicity

Other Books of Related Interest:

Opposing Viewpoints Series

Culture Wars

Discrimination

Human Rights

Current Controversies

Censorship

Hate Crimes

At Issue Series

Do Religious Groups in America Experience Discrimination?

Is the United States Ready for a Minority President?

Race and Ethnicity

Uma Kukathas, Book Editor

GREENHAVEN PRESS

An imprint of Thomson Gale, a part of The Thomson Corporation

Detroit • New York • San Francisco • New Haven, Conn. • Waterville, Maine • London

THOMSON
GALE

Christine Nasso, *Publisher*
Elizabeth Des Chenes, *Managing Editor*

© 2008 The Gale Group.

Star logo is a trademark and Gale and Greenhaven Press are registered trademarks used herein under license.

For more information, contact:
Greenhaven Press
27500 Drake Rd.
Farmington Hills, MI 48331-3535
Or you can visit our Internet site at http://www.gale.com

Articles in Greenhaven Press anthologies are often edited for length to meet page require-ments. In addition, original titles of these works are changed to clearly present the main thesis and to explicitly indicate the author's opinion. Every effort is made to ensure that Greenhaven Press accurately reflects the original intent of the authors. Every effort has been made to trace the owners of copyrighted material.

Cover photograph reproduced by permission of © Richard T. Nowitz/Corbis

LIBRARY OF CONGRESS CATALOGING-IN-PUBLICATION DATA

Race and ethnicity / Uma Kukathas, book editor.
p. cm. -- (Contemporary issues companion)
Includes bibliographical references and index.
ISBN-13: 978-0-7377-3257-3 (hardcover)
ISBN-13: 978-0-7377-3258-0 (pbk.)
1. Racism--United States. 2. Ethnicity--United States. 3. Racism in mass media.
4. Racism in popular culture. 5. United States--Race relations. 6. United States
--ethnic relations. I. Kukathas, Uma. II. Title. III. Series.
E185.615.R15 2008 2008
305.800973--dc22

2007032285

ISBN-10: 0-7377-3257-1 (hardcover)
ISBN-10: 0-7377-3258-X (pbk.)

Printed in the United States of America
10 9 8 7 6 5 4 3 2 1

Contents

Chapter 3: Race and U.S. Institutions

Chapter 4: Race and Ethnicity in the Arts and Media

Chapter 5: Reflections on Race and Ethnic Identity

Foreword

In the news, on the streets, and in neighborhoods, individuals are confronted with a variety of social problems. Such problems may affect people directly: A young woman may struggle with depression, suspect a friend of having bulimia, or watch a loved one battle cancer. And even the issues that do not directly affect her private life—such as religious cults, domestic violence, or legalized gambling—still impact the larger society in which she lives. Discovering and analyzing the complexities of issues that encompass communal and societal realms as well as the world of personal experience is a valuable educational goal in the modern world.

Effectively addressing social problems requires familiarity with a constantly changing stream of data. Becoming well informed about today's controversies is an intricate process that often involves reading myriad primary and secondary sources, analyzing political debates, weighing various experts' opinions—even listening to firsthand accounts of those directly affected by the issue. For students and general observers, this can be a daunting task because of the sheer volume of information available in books, periodicals, on the evening news, and on the Internet. Researching the consequences of legalized gambling, for example, might entail sifting through congressional testimony on gambling's societal effects, examining private studies on Indian gaming, perusing numerous Web sites devoted to Internet betting, and reading essays written by lottery winners as well as interviews with recovering compulsive gamblers. Obtaining valuable information can be time-consuming—since it often requires researchers to pore over numerous documents and commentaries before discovering a source relevant to their particular investigation.

Greenhaven's Contemporary Issues Companion series seeks to assist this process of research by providing readers with useful and pertinent information about today's complex issues. Each volume in this anthology series focuses on a topic of current interest, presenting informative and thought-provoking selections written from a wide variety of viewpoints. The readings selected by the editors include such diverse sources as personal accounts and case studies, pertinent factual and statistical articles, and relevant commentaries and overviews. This diversity of sources and views, found in every Contemporary Issues Companion, offers readers a broad perspective in one convenient volume.

In addition, each title in the Contemporary Issues Companion series is designed especially for young adults. The selections included in every volume are chosen for their accessibility and are expertly edited in consideration of both the reading and comprehension levels of the audience. The structure of the anthologies also enhances accessibility. An introductory essay places each issue in context and provides helpful facts such as historical background or current statistics and legislation that pertain to the topic. The chapters that follow organize the material and focus on specific aspects of the book's topic. Every essay is introduced by a brief summary of its main points and biographical information about the author. These summaries aid in comprehension and can also serve to direct readers to material of immediate interest and need. Finally, a comprehensive index allows readers to efficiently scan and locate content.

The Contemporary Issues Companion series is an ideal launching point for research on a particular topic. Each anthology in the series is composed of readings taken from an extensive gamut of resources, including periodicals, newspapers, books, government documents, the publications of private and public organizations, and Internet Web sites. In these volumes, readers will find factual support suitable for use in reports, debates, speeches, and research papers. The anthologies also facilitate further research, featuring a book and periodical bibliography and a list of organizations to contact for additional information.

A perfect resource for both students and the general reader, Greenhaven's Contemporary Issues Companion series is sure to be a valued source of current, readable information on social problems that interest young adults. It is the editors' hope that readers will find the Contemporary Issues Companion series useful as a starting point to formulate their own opinions about and answers to the complex issues of the present day.

Introduction

In 1857 the U.S. Supreme Court turned down a petition from Dred Scott, an enslaved African American seeking to sue his master for his freedom. Chief Justice Roger B. Taney, in delivering the majority opinion, wrote that Scott had no right to bring any suit to the federal courts, because blacks were not lawful citizens and could never be granted civil rights or equal protection under the law. Further, members of "the unhappy black race," declared Taney, were inferior to whites and thus forever "doomed to slavery."

One hundred and fifty years later, attitudes toward and the discussion about race in the United States have changed radically. From the Emancipation Proclamation in 1863 to the 1964 Civil Rights Act, enormous progress has been made, so that all races now enjoy rights of citizenship and are entitled to full legal protections. The alleged "inferiority" of blacks is thoroughly discredited, as are notions of white "supremacy." Racially discriminatory speech and practices restricting where nonwhites can live, work, and go to school are prohibited. Illustrating the profound changes that have taken place, when in February 2007 Barack Obama, a Harvard-educated lawyer, senator, and African American, declared his candidacy for president, he was immediately viewed as a front-runner for the Democratic nomination. Chief Justice Taney's grim prediction, it seems, could not have been more wrong.

Progress, but Racial Inequalities Persist

Yet, despite these remarkable gains, race continues to be the United States' most difficult and divisive social issue. Even as an African American pursues the country's highest elected office, racial inequalities and tensions persist in American life. Studies consistently show that minorities still face far greater obstacles than whites when it comes to employment, education, and health care. Statistics indicate that the poverty rate for black, Hispanic, and Native Americans is triple that of whites. Nonwhites are more likely to be incarcerated, more likely to drop out of school, and less likely to own a home. Racial profiling, the dismantling of affirmative action, hate speech, and the portrayal of minorities in the media rank as some of the country's most socially charged issues. Racially tinged incidents continue to take place, as seen in race riots in Cincinnati, Ohio, in 2001 and in Benton Harbor, Michigan, in 2003.

And while Senator Obama's successes are indicative of how far the nation has progressed, the hurdles he faces show too how much work remains to be done. Even as pundits acknowledge Obama to be one of the most intelligent and charismatic candidates to take the national stage, attention has focused on his race. First, questions arose about his ethnic identity. As the son of a white American mother and black Kenyan father, it was asked, could he show he is "black enough" to win the support of the African American community? When it was discovered that some of his mother's ancestors may have been slaveowners, several commentators argued this was evidence that he was not a "true" African American. Another storm erupted when Senator Joseph Biden referred to Obama as "the first mainstream African American who is articulate and bright and clean." And then, less than three months after announcing his candidacy, Obama was placed under the protection of the Secret Service security detail because of racist threats.

On one hand, then, the United States has made great strides in regard to its attitudes toward race and ethnicity. But on the other hand, race continues to be a difficult issue that affects the country's social and economic stability. This sense of the country having moved forward while remaining crippled by its past mistakes is a pervasive problem. One recent event illustrates exactly how strained the country's relationship is toward race and reveals that, despite legislative changes, race remains at the forefront of daily life.

Hurricane Katrina: Racism Exposed?

In August 2005 Hurricane Katrina struck the Gulf Coast of the United States, causing destruction in cities in Alabama, Mississippi, and Louisiana. Particularly hard hit was New Orleans, which flooded when nearly every single levee in the city was breached. Across the world, people viewed the images on television of a city devastated, its citizens homeless, and its government paralyzed. They also saw that, overwhelmingly, the victims of the tragedy were poor, and black. Footage shown was of black people stuck in their houses, wading through filthy floodwaters with floating corpses to help their loved ones, and trapped in the Louisiana Superdome awaiting rescue that was slow to come.

Different groups had different reactions to the media coverage. For many black leaders, the images exposed the deep-seated racial and economic problems that had long besieged New Orleans and the country as a whole. Many argued that it revealed the inequalities that had existed beyond the tourist spots of the French Quarter and Garden District but that had gone unnoticed: black people living in desperate poverty without the means to escape their plight. They contended that it showed how race and poverty in that city, and the entire country, are highly correlated, but largely ignored. Black leaders also complained that the media in its portrayals of the desperate situation had played into stereotypes by referring to white people as "finding" food while black people doing the same were said to be "looting."

Black members of Congress expressed anger at the slow federal reaction to Katrina, and many charged that race was a factor in the sluggish response. The rap artist Kanye West ignited controversy when he declared that the situation was as dire as it was because "George Bush doesn't care about black people." The event sparked a national debate about race in America, and the months afterward saw discussions in the media about poverty and racial inequality. Joining the conversation, Obama pointed out the link he saw between Katrina and the legacy of race in the country: "I hope we realize that the people of New Orleans weren't just abandoned during the hurricane. They were abandoned long ago—to murder and mayhem in the streets, to substandard schools, to dilapidated housing, to inadequate health care, to a pervasive sense of hopelessness."

For many white commentators, however, the images of Katrina's aftermath did not call up racial issues; race was not viewed by the white community as the defining factor in the tragedy and its mishandling. For some whites, the real issues were poverty and the failure of the Bush administration to heed warnings that such a disaster could strike. Many pointed out too that the large numbers of black victims seen on television were due to the population demographics of the city, and that it could not be claimed that one race suffered disproportionately in the tragedy.

The discussion prompted by Katrina soon fizzled, ironically because of these divisions along racial lines. Whites and nonwhites simply perceived the issue differently. A national survey showed that seven out of ten blacks said the disaster showed that racial inequality remains a major problem, while six out of ten whites said this was not an important lesson of the disaster. A Pew Research Center poll found that two-thirds of African Americans said the government's response to the crisis would have been faster if most of the victims had been white, while 77 percent of whites disagreed. As many news analysts, both black and white, pointed out, the disaster and its aftermath was an unfortunate reminder that dialogue about race in the United States is fraught with tension and, because of deep differences in outlooks between different ethnic groups, resolution is rarely achieved.

The Legacy of a Racialized Past

A century and a half after Dred Scott, it cannot be denied that significant racial progress has been made in the United States. The last 150 years have witnessed struggles by minorities to win the freedom and equality promised by the U.S. Constitution, and numerous legislative victories have granted them complete equality before the law. The country is more integrated than even half a century ago, as people of all races interact socially and in the workplace. Considering its troubled racial history—from the usurpation of Native American lands to the use of blacks for slave labor to the tacit assumption for five centuries of white superiority in institutions and daily life—the United States has come far.

But events such as Katrina make clear that below the surface, racial animosities continue to foment, and despite important advances, Americans still have not come to grips with its racialized past. Katrina prompted some critics to argue that in the twenty-first century, minorities are still second-class citizens who for all practical purposes do not enjoy the full complement of rights taken for granted by whites. For these critics, Chief Justice Taney's dire 1857 outlook is not so far from the truth. For others, however, hope remains, even if complete success is a long way off—commentators suggest that what is required to transform race relations are deep institutional changes, and these will take time. But in the meantime, these analysts assert, encouraging, if imperfect, signs, such as the presidential bid of a strong black candidate, might help to light the way by initiating honest and sustained dialogue among Americans about race.

CHAPTER 1

Race Classification and Ethnic Identity

The Biology of Race

Michael J. Bamshad and Steve E. Olson

Michael J. Bamshad, MD, is a geneticist and pediatrician. Steve E. Olson is a science writer whose book Mapping Human History: Genes, Race, and Our Common Origins *was a National Book Award finalist. In the following viewpoint, they ask how valid the concept of race is from a biological standpoint. The authors explain that the outward signs on which most definitions of race are based—such as skin color and hair texture—are dictated by a handful of genes. But the other genes of two people of the same "race" can be very different. Conversely, two people of different "races" can share more genetic similarity than two individuals of the same race. Nevertheless, the authors show, scientists can use genetics to sort most large populations according to their ancestral geographic origin, although this approach does not work as well for populations resulting from recent mixing with other groups. They conclude by saying that while the medical implications of racial genetic differences are still under debate, the research findings about the genetics of race take us closer to understanding where human groups are from and how they are related to one another.*

Look around on the streets of any major city, and you will see a sampling of the outward variety of humanity: skin tones ranging from milk-white to dark brown; hair textures running the gamut from fine and stick-straight to thick and wiry. People often use physical characteristics such as these—along with area of geographic origin and shared culture—to group themselves and others into "races." But how valid is the concept of race from a biological standpoint? Do physical features reliably say anything informative about a person's genetic makeup beyond indicating that the individual has genes for blue eyes or curly hair?

The problem is hard in part because the implicit definition of what makes a person a member of a particular race differs from region to region across the globe. Someone classified as "black" in the U.S., for instance, might be considered "white" in Brazil and "colored" (a category distinguished from both "black" and "white") in South Africa.

Yet common definitions of race do sometimes work well to divide groups according to genetically determined propensities for certain diseases. Sickle cell disease is usually found among people of largely African or Mediterranean descent, for instance, whereas cystic fibrosis is far more common among those of European ancestry. In addition, although the results have been controversial, a handful of studies have suggested that African-Americans are more likely to respond poorly to some drugs for cardiac disease than are members of other groups.

Over the past few years, scientists have collected data about the genetic constitution of populations around the world in an effort to probe the link between ancestry and patterns of disease. These data are now providing answers to several highly emotional and contentious questions: Can genetic information be used to distinguish human groups having a common heritage and to assign individuals to particular ones? Do such groups correspond well to predefined descriptions now widely used to specify race? And, more practically, does dividing people by familiar racial definitions or by genetic similarities say anything useful about how members of those groups experience disease or respond to drug treatment?

In general, we would answer the first question yes, the second no, and offer a qualified yes to the third. Our answers rest on several generalizations about race and genetics. Some groups do differ genetically from others, but how groups are divided depends on which genes are examined; simplistically put, you might fit into one group based on your skin-color genes but another based on a different characteristic. Many studies have demonstrated that roughly 90 percent of human genetic variation occurs within a population living on a given continent, whereas about 10 percent of the variation distinguishes continental populations. In other words, individuals from different populations are, on average, just slightly more different from one another than are individuals from the same population. Human populations are very similar, but they often can be distinguished.

Classifying Humans

As a first step to identifying links between social definitions of race and genetic heritage, scientists need a way to divide groups reliably according to their ancestry. Over the past 100,000 years or so, anatomically modern humans have migrated from Africa to other parts of the world, and members of our species have increased dramatically in number. This spread has left a distinct signature in our DNA.

To determine the degree of relatedness among groups, geneticists rely on tiny variations, or polymorphisms, in the DNA—specifically in the sequence of base pairs, the building blocks of DNA. Most of these polymorphisms do not occur within genes, the stretches of DNA that encode the information for making proteins (the molecules that constitute much of our bodies and carry out the chemical reactions of life). Accordingly, these common variations are neutral, in that they do not directly affect a particular trait. Some polymorphisms do occur in genes, however; these can contribute to individual variation in traits and to genetic diseases.

As scientists have sequenced the human genome (the full set of nuclear DNA), they have also identified millions of polymorphisms. The distribution of these polymorphisms across populations reflects the history of those populations and the effects of natural selection. To distinguish among groups, the ideal genetic polymorphism would be one that is present in all the members of one group and absent in the members of all other groups. But the major human groups have separated from one another too recently and have mixed too much for such differences to exist.

Polymorphisms that occur at different frequencies around the world can, however, be used to sort people roughly into groups. One useful class of polymorphisms consists of the Alus, short pieces of DNA that are similar in sequence to one another. Alus replicate occasionally, and the resulting copy splices itself at random into a new position on the original chromosome or on another chromosome, usually in a location that has no effect on the functioning of nearby genes. Each insertion is a unique event. Once an Alu sequence inserts itself, it can remain in place for eons, getting passed from one person to his or her descendants. Therefore, if two people have the same Alu sequence at the same spot in their genome, they must be descended from a common ancestor who gave them that specific segment of DNA.

One of us (Bamshad), working with University of Utah scientists Lynn B. Jorde, Stephen Wooding and W. Scott Watkins and with Mark A. Batzer of Louisiana State University, examined 100 different Alu polymorphisms in 565 people born in sub-Saharan Africa, Asia and Europe. First we determined the presence or absence of the 100 Alus in each of the 565 people. Next we removed all the identifying labels (such as place of origin and ethnic group) from the data and sorted the people into groups using only their genetic information.

Results of Genetic Analysis

Our analysis yielded four different groups. When we added the labels back to see whether each individual's group assignment correlated to common, predefined labels for race or ethnicity, we saw that two of the groups consisted only of individuals from sub-Saharan Africa, with one of those two made up almost entirely of Mbuti Pygmies. The other two groups consisted only of individuals from Europe and East Asia, respectively. We found that we needed 60 Alu polymorphisms to assign individuals to their continent of origin with 90 percent accuracy. To achieve nearly 100 percent accuracy, however, we needed to use about 100 Alus.

Other studies have produced comparable results. Noah A. Rosenberg and Jonathan K. Pritchard, geneticists formerly in the laboratory of Marcus W. Feldman of Stanford University, assayed approximately 375 polymorphisms called short tandem repeats in more than 1,000 people from 52 ethnic groups in Africa, Asia, Europe and the Americas. By looking at the varying frequencies of these polymorphisms, they were able to distinguish five different groups of people whose ancestors were typically isolated by oceans, deserts or mountains: sub-Saharan Africans; Europeans and Asians west of the Himalayas; East Asians; inhabitants of New Guinea and Melanesia; and Native Americans. They were also able to identify subgroups within each region that usually corresponded with each member's self-reported ethnicity.

The results of these studies indicate that genetic analyses can distinguish groups of people according to their geographic origin. But caution is warranted. The groups easiest to resolve were those that were widely separated from one another geographically. Such samples maximize the genetic variation among groups. When Bamshad and his co-workers used their 100 Alu polymorphisms to try to classify a sample of individuals from southern India into a separate group, the Indians instead had more in common with either Europeans or Asians. In other words, because India has been subject to many genetic influences from Europe and Asia, people on the subcontinent did not group into a unique cluster. We concluded that many hundreds—or perhaps thousands—of polymorphisms might have to be examined to distinguish between groups whose ancestors have historically interbred with multiple populations.

The Human Race

Given that people can be sorted broadly into groups using genetic data, do common notions of race correspond to underlying genetic differences among populations? In some cases they do, but often they do not. For instance, skin color or facial features—traits influenced by natural selection—are routinely used to divide people into races. But groups with similar physical characteristics as a result of selection can be quite different genetically. Individuals from sub-Saharan Africa and Australian Aborigines might have similar skin pigmentation (because of adapting to strong sun), but genetically they are quite dissimilar.

In contrast, two groups that are genetically similar to each other might be exposed to different selective forces. In this case, natural selection can exaggerate some of the differences between groups, making them appear more dissimilar on the surface than they are underneath. Because traits such as skin color have been strongly affected by natural selection, they do not necessarily reflect the population processes that have shaped the distribution of neutral polymorphisms such as Alus or short tandem repeats. Therefore, traits or polymorphisms affected by natural selection may be poor predictors of group membership and may imply genetic relatedness where, in fact, little exists.

Another example of how difficult it is to categorize people involves populations in the U.S. Most people who describe themselves as African-American have relatively recent ancestors from West Africa, and West Africans generally have polymorphism frequencies that can be distinguished from those of Europeans, Asians and Native Americans. The fraction of gene variations that African-Americans share with West Africans, however, is far from uniform, because over the centuries African-Americans have mixed extensively with groups originating from elsewhere in Africa and beyond.

Over the past several years, Mark D. Shriver of Pennsylvania State University and Rick A. Kittles of Howard University have defined a set of polymorphisms that they have used to estimate the fraction of a person's genes originating from each continental region. They found that the West African contribution to the genes of individual African-Americans averages about 80 percent, although it ranges from 20 to 100 percent. Mixing of groups is also apparent in many individuals who believe they have only European ancestors. According to Shriver's analyses, approximately 30 percent of Americans who consider themselves "white" have less than 90 percent European ancestry. Thus, self-reported ancestry is not necessarily a good predictor of the genetic composition of a large number of Americans. Accordingly, common notions of race do not always reflect a person's genetic background.

Membership Has Its Privileges

Understanding the relation between race and genetic variation has important practical implications. Several of the polymorphisms that differ in frequency from group to group have specific effects on health. The mutations responsible for sickle cell disease and some cases of cystic fibrosis, for instance, result from genetic changes that appear to have risen in frequency because they were protective against diseases prevalent in Africa and Europe, respectively. People who inherit one copy of the sickle cell polymorphism show some resistance to malaria; those with one copy of the cystic fibrosis trait may be less prone to the dehydration resulting from cholera. The symptoms of these diseases arise only in the unfortunate individuals who inherit two copies of the mutations.

Genetic variation also plays a role in individual susceptibility to one of the worst scourges of our age: AIDS. Some people have a small deletion in both their copies of a gene that encodes a particular cell-surface receptor called chemokine receptor 5 (CCR5). As a result, these individuals fail to produce CCR5 receptors on the surface of their cells. Most strains of HIV-1, the virus that causes AIDS, bind to the CCR5 receptor to gain entry to cells, so people who lack CCR5 receptors are resistant to HIV-1 infection. This polymorphism in the CCR5 receptor gene is found almost exclusively in groups from northeastern Europe.

Several polymorphisms in CCR5 do not prevent infection but instead influence the rate at which HIV-1 infection leads to AIDS and death. Some of these polymorphisms have similar effects in different populations; others only alter the speed of disease progression in selected groups. One polymorphism, for example, is associated with delayed disease progression in European-Americans but accelerated disease in African-Americans. Researchers can only study such population-specific effects—and use that knowledge to direct therapy—if they can sort people into groups.

In these examples—and others like them—a polymorphism has a relatively large effect in a given disease. If genetic screening were inexpensive and efficient, all individuals could be screened for all such disease-related gene variants. But genetic testing remains costly. Perhaps more significantly, genetic screening raises concerns about privacy and consent: some people might not want to know about genetic factors that could increase their risk of developing a particular disease. Until these issues are resolved further, self-reported ancestry will continue to be a potentially useful diagnostic tool for physicians.

Ancestry may also be relevant for some diseases that are widespread in particular populations. Most common diseases, such as hypertension and diabetes, are the cumulative results of polymorphisms in several genes, each of which has a small influence on its own. Recent research suggests that polymorphisms that have a particular effect in one group may have a different effect in another group. This kind of complexity would make it much more difficult to use detected polymorphisms as a guide to therapy. Until further studies are done on the genetic and environmental contributions to complex diseases, physicians may have to rely on information about an individual's ancestry to know how best to treat some diseases.

Race and Medicine

But the importance of group membership as it relates to health care has been especially controversial in recent years. Last January [2003] the U.S. Food and Drug Administration [FDA] issued guidelines advocating the collection of race and ethnicity data in all clinical trials. Some investigators contend that the differences between groups are so small and the historical abuses associated with categorizing people by race so extreme that group membership should play little if any role in genetic and medical studies. They assert that the FDA should abandon its recommendation and instead ask researchers conducting clinical trials to collect genomic data on each individual. Others suggest that only by using group membership, including common definitions of race based on skin color, can we understand how genetic and environmental differences among groups contribute to disease. This debate will be settled only by further research on the validity of race as a scientific variable.

A set of articles in the March 20 [2003] issue of the *New England Journal of Medicine* debated both sides of the medical implications of race. The authors of one article—Richard S. Cooper of the Loyola Stritch School of Medicine, Jay S. Kaufman of the University of North Carolina at Chapel Hill and Ryk Ward of the University of Oxford—argued that race is not an adequate criterion for physicians to use in choosing a particular drug for a given patient. They pointed out two findings of racial differences that are both now considered questionable: that a combination of certain blood vessel–dilating drugs was more effective in treating heart failure in people of African ancestry and that specific enzyme inhibitors (angiotensin converting enzyme, or ACE, inhibitors) have little efficacy in such individuals. In the second article, a group led by Neil Risch of Stanford University countered that racial or ethnic groups can differ from one another genetically and that the differences can have medical importance. They cited a study showing that the rate of complications from type 2 diabetes varies according to race, even after adjusting for such factors as disparities in education and income.

The intensity of these arguments reflects both scientific and social factors. Many biomedical studies have not rigorously defined group membership, relying instead on inferred relationships based on racial categories. The dispute over the importance of group membership also illustrates how strongly the perception of race is shaped by different social and political perspectives.

In cases where membership in a geographically or culturally defined group has been correlated with health-related genetic traits, knowing something about an individual's group membership could be important for a physician. And to the extent that human groups live in different environments or have different experiences that affect health, group membership could also reflect nongenetic factors that are medically relevant.

Regardless of the medical implications of the genetics of race, the research findings are inherently exciting. For hundreds of years, people have wondered where various human groups came from and how those groups are related to one another. They have speculated about why human populations have different physical appearances and about whether the biological differences between groups are more than skin deep. New genetic data and new methods of analysis are finally allowing us to approach these questions. The result will be a much deeper understanding of both our biological nature and our human interconnectedness.

Biology Is Not the Only Determination of Race

Kimberly TallBear

Kimberly TallBear is an assistant professor of American Indian studies at the University of Arizona. In the following essay, she finds that race as a natural division among human populations has been largely discredited by scientists. But, she declares, this view of race as a fixed division among people is perpetuated in the racialization of American Indian tribes and American Indian ethnicity. She finds particularly troubling the efforts to use biological tests, including DNA analysis to test for genetic markers, to measure who is "truly Indian"—this is reminiscent of the nineteenth-century eugenics movement, she says. TallBear also states that Indian activists, scholars, and writers, by asserting racialized images of their people in order to underscore collective tribal practices and beliefs, should be careful not to reinforce the role of blood in assertions of cultural and political authority.

I saw American broadcaster Larry King interview African-American comedian Chris Rock in February 2001 on CNN International. King asked Rock how he felt about recent developments related to mapping the human genome. When Chris Rock appeared puzzled and responded more or less that he didn't feel qualified to address the topic, King elaborated that such scientific inquiry might be used to make black people white and didn't Mr. Rock have an opinion about this? Recognizing King's unfamiliarity with the psychology of race, Chris Rock seemed to see that this was one battle in which he didn't want to engage on international television. He responded graciously and with a smile, "It isn't like that."

Kimberly TallBear, "DNA, Blood, and Racializing the Tribe," *Wicazo Sa Review*, vol. 18, spring 2003, pp. 81–107. Reproduced by permission of the author.

Race: Biology Versus Ideology

Larry King is a long-standing commentator on U.S. American political life, and race has been called "the most explosive issue in American life." King's comments illustrate that there is little societal familiarity with how race is constructed as ideology. It is thought to be biological fact. The progressive work of activists and scholars has shed much light on race as ideology—as a social construction that is "the product of specific historical and geographical forces, rather than [a] biologically given [idea] whose meaning is dictated by nature." Although race as natural division in human populations has been widely discredited in science, it is so integral to the way that many people think that it is still considered a natural and fixed human division. Such views of race have been much critiqued in studies of the invention of the white race and its systematic oppression of other races. . . .

This essay is intended to shed light on racialized ideas of "Indianness" and how such ideas actually undermine tribal political and cultural authority. Tribal people, our advocates, and scientists (despite unexamined assumptions about scientific objectivity) have not escaped the influence of racial ideology; the racialized perspective is represented as DNA (with the aura of technological finality) in a metaphor of blood or perpetuated in more insidious ways such as racialized and romanticized images of Indians.

A Note on the Tribal Nation

The idea that tribes possessed political autonomy, or nationhood, before the arrival of newcomers from Europe is deeply entrenched among tribes and in federal government policy language. The conflicts that arise in tribal enrollment are a result of tribes desiring to protect their cultural, geographic, and political authorities. Tribes consider such authorities to be at the heart of what determines their status as unique peoples or nations with the right to govern themselves. The Bureau of

Indian Affairs (BIA) describes "membership in an Indian tribe, band, or colony [is] different from membership in any ... *volutary association of people*. Membership in an Indian tribe, band or colony is like citizenship in a country." Both tribes and the federal government view tribal membership as a fundamental exercise of tribal governance and signifier of tribal nationhood. Often, tribes assert nationhood in the face of what they view as disrespect for or misunderstanding of their *cultural and political authority*. Blood talk and, increasingly, talk of DNA have unfortunately infiltrated tribal political life and are used to help justify cultural and political authority. Such biological measures reaffirm racial definitions of the tribal nation and who rightly claims tribal citizenship. The following is a discussion of how such attempts to protect cultural authority actually undermine that authority.

Native American DNA?

Before delving into a discussion of DNA analysis and native identity, it seems appropriate to briefly explain the science that is misused to support the political act of asserting or disputing such identity and attendant political and cultural claims. An informative briefing paper that explains and disputes genetic markers as a valid test of native identity was issued by the Nevada-based Indigenous Peoples Council on Biocolonialism (IPCB). It summarizes for laypeople the theory used to support genetics as an indicator of Native American identity. A brief passage conveys the basic science:

> Scientists have found certain ... "markers" in human genes that they call Native American markers because they believe all "original" Native Americans had these genetic traits.... The markers are principally analyzed in two locations in people's genes—in their mitochondrial DNA and on the Y-chromosome. On the mitochondrial DNA, there are a total of five different "haplotypes" ... which are increasingly called "Native American markers," and are believed to be a

genetic signature of the founding ancestors. As for the Y-chromosome, there are two primary lineages or "haplo-groups" that are seen in modern Native American groups. . . . It must be pointed out that none of these markers is exclusive to Native American populations—all can be found in other populations around the world. They simply occur with more frequency in Native American populations.

. . . Tribes, at least rhetorically, claim to organize themselves according to their inherent sovereignty and the idea of the tribal nation. If this is the goal, then racializing the tribe (naming that entity as only a biological entity) undermines both tribal cultural and political authorities. Although blood quantum, as it is practiced today, has some historical roots in other philosophies, tribal cultural and political self-determination is not well served by basing citizenship and cultural affiliation solely in narrow policies of biological kinship. Tribal ideas of kinship and community belonging are not synonymous with biology. If tribal political practice is not meaningfully informed by cultural practice and philosophy, it seems that tribes are abdicating self-determination. This is not to suggest that any tribe can or should revolutionize its citizenship practices overnight. A bit of history and a couple of stories that illustrate contemporary problems associated with basing tribal citizenship and cultural affiliation in DNA or blood quantum follow. . . .

The Politics of Blood Quantum

If the use of DNA analysis to determine cultural affiliation is troubling because of its racial implications, the use by tribes of blood quantum to determine eligibility for citizenship cannot be ignored. It seems clear that DNA analysis for such a purpose is not a new political concept, but simply reinforces a historical practice of both the U.S. government and federally recognized tribes.

Since the late 1800s, blood quantum has been used by the U.S. Department of the Interior, the BIA, and many tribal governments to determine eligibility (although not always as a sole criterion) for tribal membership and benefits. It has been reported that the inception of federal identification policies for American Indians based on racialized notions of blood were first instituted in treaties and subsequently reinforced or reaffirmed by the General Allotment Act of 1887 (the Dawes Act). Others have disputed how clearly such a practice was mandated and suggest that the Dawes Act did not explicitly require the measure of blood quantum. Rather, the Dawes Act required that tribal group members be defined for the purpose of allotting Indian tribal property to individuals. And this requirement was interpreted by the Department of the Interior (home of the BIA) to support its existing ideology of using blood quantum as a determinant of tribal affiliation. . . .

Many critics characterize blood quantum policies as solely representing Euro-American definitions of race imposed on native peoples by the U.S. government. Ward Churchill, a vocal critic of blood quantum policies, has asserted that

> virtually every indigenous nation within the United States had, by way of an unrelenting substitution of federal definitions for their own, been stripped of the ability to determine for themselves in any meaningful way the internal composition of their politics.

Churchill argues that tribes were forced to adopt racial codes that linked identity to quantities of Indian blood and that such ideology was "psychologically and intellectually internalized by Native America," a self-imposed "sort of autogenocide by definitional and statistical extermination."

On the other hand, a handful of scholars have argued that the historical politics of blood quantum are more complex than is usually reported. Alexandra Harmon provides an insightful analysis that reveals the complexity of the politics involved in the Colville Reservation Indians' symbolic, strategic, and contradictory use of blood quantum historically to help determine eligibility of individuals for tribal affiliation and allotment of lands:

> Government agents apparently saw a need to teach Indians the basic qualifications for membership in a U.S.-supervised tribe. They announced ground rules for enrollment and overrode some Indian council decisions for failing to comport with those rules. They insisted that ancestry—metaphorically termed "Indian blood"—be one of those qualifications, and they argued on several occasions that excluding people with a low Indian "blood quantum" would protect the economic interests of Indians already on the roll. Some council members adopted this line.

> However, the Coleville documents tell a more complex, ambiguous story than [some blood quantum critics and advocates] do. In the enrollment councils, federal agents did not brainwash or impose their will on Indians; neither did Indians resolve to draw an economically strategic, racially defined boundary around themselves. Rather, officials and Indians participated in a prolonged discourse that I would characterize as incomplete mutual education and accommodation.

This scholar argues that "to provide a sounder foundation for conclusions about the influence of U.S. law and racial ideology on the composition of tribes, more historical studies [grounded in specific tribal membership histories] are essential." Without such historically grounded studies, she suggests that claims that tribes are ubiquitously forced or duped into acceptance of Euro-American racial ideology are conjecture. Harmon concludes that tribal enrollment efforts in the early 1900s prompted "an unprecedented conversation—one that would take place in many tribal communities and continue for decades—about what it meant to be Indian in the twentieth-century United States"....

Pauline Turner Strong and Barrik Van Winkle have similarly discussed the interplay in the works of certain tribal writers between literal and metaphorical interpretations of blood and "positive" uses of blood imagery, such as using it as "a vehicle of connection and integration . . . rather than one of calculation and differentiation." . . .

These scholars attempt to do justice to the complexity of blood quantum politics among Indian peoples. Yet in the final analysis, [scholar Melissa L.] Meyer zeros in on the implications for tribes of maintaining the practice of measurement and thus accepting the racial ideology (and its attendant economic benefits) implied in U.S. federal practice:

> In their purest form, blood quantum requirements amount to a celebration of race. But turning the tables in this fashion, though it may have accorded to some degree with their own notions of "blood" and lineage, would not spare tribes or individuals from the destructive consequences of basing policies on racial criteria.

"Blood" Undermines Kinship

There are potentially profound losses for communities as a result of imposing racialized standards for citizenship in tribal nations—whether those standards are imposed in keeping with restrictions posed by the U.S. government or whether they are the result of internal tribal dialogues and negotiations. While racial requirements are unofficial factors in the citizenship policies of some nations (i.e., as in discrimination in favor of certain types of immigrants and against others based on perceived racial characteristics), nonracial requirements are more often held to officially determine citizenship. Tribes also had nonracial requirements before European and Euro-American colonization. Some of these persisted officially into the twentieth century, and many persist unofficially. They include being born within the tribal community, marrying or being adopted into the community, long-term residence within the tribal community, and the assumption of cultural norms such as language, religion, and other practices.

My great-grandmother, Agnes Dauphine, was born in 1906 to Métis (French and Chippewa descent) parents in Saskatchewan, Canada. She married my great-grandfather, Felix Heminger, in the 1920s, and they moved to where some of his people were in Flandreau, South Dakota (today the Flandreau Santee Sioux Tribe Reservation). In 1941, she was adopted into the tribe. My great-grandmother had studied the Dakota language in order to speak with her mother-in-law and other relatives, and lived and worked in Flandreau for most of her adult life. With my great-grandfather she brought four children into the tribal community. They also had eleven grandchildren and twenty-plus great-grandchildren, most of whom live there and are tribal members. When my great-grandmother died in 1995, she was the eldest tribal member. While tribal enrollment records indicate that her "1/2 Chippewa Indian blood" was a factor in her enrollment in Flandreau, it is significant that the tribal enrollment ordinance in effect at the time provided for adoptions into the tribe of adopted children and spouses of tribal members, regardless of Flandreau Santee Sioux blood. This is no longer the case.

Like the Colville Tribe example, the Flandreau Santee Sioux in the first half of the twentieth century can be seen to have negotiated where the line fell between tribal ideas of kin and government ideas of blood measurement. However, contemporary enrollment standards require "1/4 or more degree of Flandreau Santee Sioux blood" or "1/4 or more total degree of Indian blood of a federally recognized Indian tribe *with an ancestral trace back to the [Flandreau Santee Sioux] Tribe's 1934 base roll*" (author's emphasis). By contemporary standards, my great-grandmother would not have been a tribal citizen.

Possible reasons for such a change in tribal policy come immediately to mind. The tribal economy has changed greatly since 1941. Throughout the 1970s and 1980s, the tribe built a health, housing, and community infrastructure that would have amazed the Flandreau Indians of the early twentieth century. In the late 1980s, they opened a casino, small by some standards, but this venture offers more jobs than tribal members alone can fill. Per capita payments (monthly payments from casino revenues) are also paid to enrolled tribal members. Instituting the Flandreau Santee Sioux blood quantum criterion might have been a strategy for warding off exploitation by individuals interested solely in financial gain rather than the cultural and political life of the community, or it might indicate the further acceptance by tribal policy makers of race-based ideology, or both. Whatever the incentives, there is clearly a potential threat to broader kin relations. Nonetheless, as the Colville scholarship indicates, specific historical research needs to be done. Without it, my assessment, though certainly informed by having lived in the community, is incomplete.

There are undoubtedly similar examples of changes in enrollment policy among tribes all over the country. But Harmon points out that the historical and specific tribal research is scanty. More such research needs to be done to reveal the broader trends among tribes during the twentieth century as they moved between tribal cultural ideas of kin and community belonging and U.S. policy that sought to influence tribal citizenship with racial ideology.

The Implications of Racializing the Tribe

Racialized (often romanticized and pan-Indian) images are common in the writing of some Indian activists, poets, scholars, politicians, and our advocates—perhaps more common than images that reinforce *specific* tribal cultural practices and beliefs. Such ideas are often intended to be flattering or sympathetic and helpful to the cause of tribes. But we should be gravely concerned that such images actually reinforce the role of blood in assertions of cultural and political authority. (Ironically, such romanticized images sometimes come from critics of blood quantum.) Romanticized, pan-Indian, and racialized approaches to tribal identity all de-emphasize specific tribal beliefs, histories, and place-based practices that are sometimes contradictory between tribes. This robs future generations of specifically applied cultural knowledge that can help guide tribes through the challenges they face.

The Colville enrollment history has demonstrated the importance of historical research related to citizenship practices as they developed in the late 1800s and early 1900s, which might also include ideas of nation or people, kinship and community as these are reflected in tribal languages, and in both historical and contemporary cultural practices associated with specific tribes. Such research can help generate new citizenship strategies that aren't racialized as well as promote culturally informed and critical governance more generally. This is not to say that tribes should work in isolation from each other. Each tribe or group of related tribes must reckon with their own history and cultural practice in relation to citizenship. But their process models for doing so can be shared between tribes to make better use of intellectual and financial resources.

On the other hand, continuing to use blood quantum and DNA analysis to claim individual or tribal cultural and political authority is a strategy that could be used against tribes to challenge such authorities. There are other strategies by which tribes might determine citizenship to better reflect tribal political authority, to encourage a thriving culture, economic investment, and social commitment to the tribal community. The specific historic practices of tribes may be a good source of ideas if they can be adapted, applied, and enforced within a contemporary sociopolitical context.

As tribes seek to build the governing infrastructures and the educational, cultural, and economic institutions that will increase tribal capacity to govern, it seems that resistance to racial ideology is imperative. We have seen in war-torn nations all over the world the horrific results of clinging to racial and essentialist views of who is an authentic member of the nation and who, therefore, deserves political, cultural, and human rights. It will be a sad turn of events if such violations are perpetuated on a smaller scale within tribal communities.

DNA Testing Provides a Link to the Past

John Simons

John Simons is a writer at Fortune *magazine, covering technology, media, the pharmaceutical industry, and general business issues. In the following essay he considers his ties, as an African American, to his African ancestors. He wonders where his ancestral lineage originates and who his people are. After emancipation, he says, most African Americans did not talk about their past and were unable to trace their ethnic heritage to a specific point of origin in Africa. But now science has made it possible for black Americans to take a genetic test that can help them determine their ancestral origins. Simons describes his thoughts after taking the controversial genetic test to learn more about his ethnic and cultural roots.*

One of the many joys of the World Cup is engaging in a 30-day frenzy of flag-hugging nationalism. Many Americans root for more than one team: the U.S. and the country of their ancestors. If you're vaguely German, your veins pop when a bad call goes against Team Germany. Third-generation Italian? Your wardrobe isn't complete without the stylish blue jersey of the Azzuri.

Every four years I pick an African team to support. Last summer it was Angola. In 1998 I was a Nigerian for a day, celebrating in a West African bar as their team upset Spain, 3–2. But I knew I was an interloper. As a black American, when the red-white-and-blue is not on the field, who is my team?

This query, of course, goes deeper than sports. Yes, I'm African American, but what does that mean? Where on the vast

12 million-square-mile continent does my ancestral lineage originate? Who are my people? I assumed those questions were unanswerable. Even the most intensive genealogical research is unlikely to tease out the ethnic and regional origins of the millions of descendents of Africans who crossed the ocean as chattel.

The Slave Trade

The reasons are myriad. During the three-century-long trade, most slaves came (and were shipped) from the far-western curve of Africa that stretches from Senegal to Nigeria. But as a result of wars, migration and trade, Africans from other parts of the continent also were captured.

Before the voyage across the Atlantic, tribe members were almost always separated to prevent them from plotting rebellion. Once they arrived on plantations, they were discouraged from practicing tribal customs.

As time went on, slaves intermarried; linguistic links were cut as they often took the last names of their owners. To further confuse the issue of genetic origin, many slave women bore white men's children, either the result of rape (a common occurrence) or more complicated relationships, such as that of Sally Hemings and Thomas Jefferson.

After emancipation, many families tried to bury the sadness of slavery, and didn't talk much about the past. All this served to create a uniquely African-American identity. But individuals were unable to trace their ethnic heritage to a point of origin in Africa itself.

Until now. Science has made it possible for black Americans (as well as blacks in the Caribbean and Latin America) to take a genetic test that can help them breach the barriers of history.

A building site provided the lever. In 1991 a construction crew digging in lower Manhattan uncovered a 17th- and 18th-century graveyard housing the remains of some 400 Africans.

Six years later Rick Kittles, a professor of genetic medicine at the University of Chicago, joined a team of Howard University scientists and historians to study the site.

Studying the Genes of African Slaves

In order to determine the origins of these black New Yorkers, Kittles took genetic samples from the remains and attempted to match them against present-day Africans. But the existing databases were too small to make credible matches. So Kittles began collecting samples himself, as well as buying and borrowing from other companies and academics. Today his 25,000-sample compilation is the world's largest storehouse of African DNA and is the cornerstone of African Ancestry Inc., the company Kittles co-founded in 2003.

"Every generation comes up with the same questions," notes Kittles, who says he had always been haunted by the mysteries of his tribal heritage. "But when we use the traditional methods other people use to research the family tree, we hit a wall. As a geneticist, I knew the wall could be overcome."

African Ancestry came along at just the right time. Some 73 percent of Americans say they are interested in researching their family history, according to a 2005 poll by Marketing Strategies Inc. That's up from roughly 50 percent a decade ago. Three factors seem to be driving this interest. First, raw historical records, such as census data and birth and death certificates, have become easier to access because of the Internet. Software has made it easier to catalog data on home computers. And finally, DNA testing has become less expensive and more readily available.

Although the history of slavery presents peculiar roadblocks—particularly poor record-keeping of slave births and deaths—African Americans are no less interested in their families' past. African Ancestry's business has doubled in each of the past four years; all told, it has served 10,000 customers.

Throughout the year, Kittles zigzags the country, giving lectures on DNA research to black churches and community groups. But business really took off in early 2006 when, as part of a PBS miniseries on the ancestral ties of African Americans, Harvard historian Henry Louis Gates Jr. used Kittles's analysis to link nine famous African Americans, including Oprah Winfrey, Quincy Jones and Whoopi Goldberg, to their African homelands.

Discovering My Past

In mid-November I decided to make the same journey and delivered genetic samples to African Ancestry's offices. I took both of the tests the company offers—an analysis of mitochondrial DNA, passed to me from my mother and her mother, and so on, and a second test to examine my Y-chromosome, passed to me from my father and his father, etc. The cost: $550.

The sample collection was simple. For each exam, I rubbed my inner cheeks and gums for two minutes, collecting microscopic tissue samples on a swab, then sealed them into separate bar-coded envelopes. The specimens would first go to a Utah DNA processor called Sorenson Genomics, which sequences, digitizes and sends the DNA to Kittles in Chicago. Using proprietary software, Kittles tries to identify matches between his clients' DNA and those in his gene database. The whole thing takes four to six weeks.

What's interesting, and somewhat limiting, about the tests is that my mitochondrial DNA can only reveal information about my mother's mother's lineage. And my Y-chromosome analysis can only provide clues about my father's father's ancestry. That's all the genetic information I carry. What's left out, then, is information about my mother's father's DNA (passed through generations via the male line), and my father's mother's DNA, which is maternally inherited.

A few days before Christmas, I received my results in the mail. "The mitochondrial [i.e., maternal] DNA sequence that we determined from your sample shares ancestry with the Mende, Temne and Limba peoples in Sierra Leone today," read my official letter. Included in the envelope was a lengthy explanation of the genetic analysis, along with a graphic depicting portions of my DNA and a booklet offering information and sources for further research on specific ethnic groups.

"The Y-chromosome DNA markers," the letter continued, "share ancestry with people in two countries today: the Makua people of Mozambique and the Lissongo people in the Central African Republic. While these groups may differ socially and culturally, there are people within them who share a common genetic ancestry."

My Slave Ancestors

Kittles helped put my ancestry in context. About 30 percent of his clients have Sierra Leone matches, he says, which makes sense, as it's in the heart of the slave-trading region. Only about 5 percent of African slaves were from what is now Mozambique and Madagascar in the southeast, far from the main centers.

With this new information in hand, I now know more about my African ancestors than I do about many succeeding generations. The entire period between when my ancestors arrived (whenever that was) and the early 20th century is a mystery.

Tracing Roots of the Family Tree

On my father's side, I know that my paternal great-grandfather was born in Brooklyn in 1910. His parents and their families, so I'm told, had lived in northern Virginia for generations. My mother's family hails from the Bahamas. Early details of their arrival in the U.S. are sketchy because they came as illegal immigrants and picked fruit in Florida. By the early 1940s, when my mother was born, they were living legally in Brooklyn.

My mother, visiting me for the holidays, couldn't contain her excitement upon hearing that she was related to the three main ethnic groups in Sierra Leone. She immediately commandeered my computer and began surfing Web sites for photos of the Mende, Limba and Temne people. "Oh, my God. She looks like Aunt Louise," she said, pointing to a photo of a Mende woman standing in a field with her children.

After a few more hours on the computer and a trip to the bookstore, my mother had a plausible theory about our Sierra Leone origins: Slaves from Sierra Leone were sought for their expertise in rice farming. Many of them ended up in the Carolinas and Georgia as the backbone of the region's rice industry. How did these possible ancestors get from the Carolinas to the Bahamas? Before the American Revolution, the Bahamas was a sparsely populated British outpost, but after the American victory in 1783, many plantation owners who remained British loyalists resettled in British colonies in the Caribbean. Between 1784 and 1789, the population of the Bahamas tripled to 12,000 people—three-quarters of them slaves.

My mother and I could not have made these kinds of connections, however tenuous, without the results from African Ancestry. But a number of scientists have questioned the interpretations the company makes (and are more than a little piqued that Kittles does not share his database). Last October, Bert Ely, a geneticist at the University of South Carolina, published a paper suggesting that African-American mitochondrial DNA has been mixed so much that, in many cases, it is impossible to find a match with a single ethnic group in Africa.

The Critics of African Ancestry Research

Ely plotted the DNA sequences of 170 African Americans against those of 3,725 people living in Africa. He found that

45

most African Americans share lineage with three or more groups of Africans. He also found that some 40 percent of African Americans had no match with Africans in his database. In my case, it's not that my DNA doesn't match the Mende, according to critics, but that I may not have the full picture.

"You're limited by the size of the database," says Jonathan Marks, an anthropologist at the University of North Carolina. "How many other people did you match from other tribes that were not sampled?" The question is fair. Still, although the record is incomplete, I now have a link to my past I did not have before.

Pilar Ossorio, a professor of bioethics and law at the University of Wisconsin, questions the claims of specificity. "Just as an example," she says, "there are people in the Balkans who share the same mitochondrial DNA with people in Africa."

Kittles defends his research. His database is more than triple the size of Ely's, he notes; therefore, it has more ethnic variability and is more accurate. He grouses, "This is sour grapes that I didn't share my data with them."

A Growing Clientele for Discovering African Ancestry

African Ancestry's clients appear unfazed. On a Web forum, customers overwhelmingly side with the company. Dwainia Tullis's view is typical. Last August she discovered she shared ancestry with the Balanta and Fulani tribes of Guinea Bissau.

"I'm getting another cousin of mine involved to cover all sides of the family," says the 51-year-old hairdresser from California. And what has been the benefit? "I'm more whole now," she says simply.

For me, my family tree is still missing branches. Rather than one specific place of belonging, I've discovered I share DNA with people spanning the entire continent of Africa. In the end, I feel more African when I peer into the mirror—and, oddly, more American.

Racial Identity and Politics

Patricia Williams

Patricia Williams, a professor of law at Columbia University and a member of the State Bar of California, writes the Nation *column "Diary of a Mad Law Professor." In the following essay, Williams argues that Barack Obama's pursuit of the presidency has caused the media to obsess over exactly how black he is, bringing into debate America's slippery notions of race, culture, and ethnicity.*

> *I mean, you got the first sort of mainstream African-American who's articulate and bright and clean and a nice-looking guy. I mean, that's a storybook, man.*
>
> —Senator Joseph Biden,
> *in faint but unfettered praise of Senator Barack Obama*

Recently the New-York Historical Society and the Studio Museum of Harlem curated "Legacies," a fascinating show at N-YHS in which contemporary artists reflected on slavery. One of the commissioned pieces that accompanied the display was a short film by artists Bradley McCallum and Jacqueline Tarry. It featured McCallum, who is white, and Tarry, who is black, configured as a "twinning doll"—a nineteenth-century toy that has two heads, one at each end of a common torso. At the doll's waist is attached a long skirt or a cloak. Held vertically, the skirt falls and obscures one head. Flipped one way, it becomes a white doll. Turned upside down, the skirt falls the other way and suddenly it's a black doll. In the film, McCallum and Tarry, joined at the waist by some feat of pixilated trickery and dressed in nineteenth-century clothing, flip head over head down a long dark marble corridor, first a white head, then a black head, first a white man, then a black

Patricia Williams, "L'Étranger," *The Nation*, February 16, 2007, Copyright © 2007 by The Nation Magazine/The Nation Company, Inc. Reproduced by permission.

woman, first a Thomas Jefferson, then a Sally Hemings. As they describe it, "the races are joined head to toe . . . continuously revealing and concealing one another." Such an interesting metaphor for the state of our union.

When I inquired further, McCallum told me that there was an old children's song about the dolls: "Turn you up/Turn you back./First you're white/Then you're black." I tried Googling those words in hopes of finding a recording. Instead I turned up a satirical piece by rocker Lou Reed, "I Wanna Be Black," in which a (presumably hypothetical) "I" desires "to be black" as an escape from a neurosis of whiteness. Actually, the word "white" is never used in the song. It's alluded to in the chorus—obliquely but with crystal clarity nonetheless: "I don't wanna be a f---ed-up middle-class college student any more." According to these lyrics, whiteness is a dull preserve defined by respectable class status, college education and world-class angst; black people have ever so much more fun, what with having "natural rhythm," "a big prick," a "stable of foxy whores" and "get myself shot in the spring" "like Martin Luther King."

"Acting White" Versus "Acting Black"

The jolly entertainment of switching identity from white to black and back again is not the exclusive province of frat boys slumming around as pretenders to ghetto life. "Jungle parties" are still good clean fun at country clubs, at Halloween parties down at the precinct and in the unfortunate confusion that is Kevin Federline. The inverse—switching from black to white and black again—is more freighted. Blacks who present themselves as clean and articulate and sober and important risk being viewed as false, elitist or duplicitous. "Acting white" has all these connotations. Whites "acting black," on the other hand— i.e., any coded masquerade of down and dirty—tend to be read as cool or maybe disaffected or, at worst, stuck in some stage of rebellious adolescence.

Frankly, what I found most unforgivable about Senator Biden's recent remarks was his utter failure to learn from a past in which he was intimately implicated. He was, after all, chair of the Senate Judiciary Committee when our spectacularly inarticulate President's [George W. Bush] father [former president George H.W. Bush] nominated Clarence Thomas to the Supreme Court. As every last minority graduate of Yale—whew, ten or fifteen at least—came forward to weigh in about whether Thomas or Anita Hill was more believable, media forces expressed shock and awe that there were—gasp—just so many black people who could string a whole sentence together! Astonishing sequences of subject-verb-object! A few years later, it was [former secretary of state] Colin Powell who was perceived as shockingly articulate; then Condoleezza Rice.

The persistence of this narrative is not limited to Biden. On MSNBC's *Chris Matthews Show*, Matthews hosted a discussion of Obama's decision to run for President. "No history of Jim Crow, no history of anger, no history of slavery," Matthews opined. "All the bad stuff in our history ain't there with this guy." Not true, I thought. The "bad stuff in our history" rests heavily upon each and every one of us. It shapes us all, whether me, Matthews, Obama, Biden—or Amadou Diallo, the decent, hard-working Guinean immigrant without any American racial "history," who died in a hail of bullets fired by New York City police officers because he looked like what the officers, groaning with racial "baggage," imagined to be a criminal. Some parts of our racial experience are nothing more or less than particular to *our* accidental location in the geography of a culture.

Obama and the History of Chosen Migration

If, for example, I migrated to South Africa and were greeted as an exciting, exotic black American prophet (we "articulate" blacks are inescapably "exotic" when we travel abroad), I'd be no less implicated in the complexities of that country's racial struggles—even if I were entirely ignorant of those struggles. At a more complex level, however. American identity is defined by the experience of the willing diaspora, the break by choice that is the heart of the immigrant myth. It is that narrative of chosen migration that has exiled most African-Americans from a substantial part of the American narrative—and it is precisely his place in that narrative that makes Obama so attractive, so intriguing and yet so strange.

Obama's family history is an assemblage of elements of the American dream. His late father migrated from Kenya to the United States; his mother was from Kansas. Before him, the archetypal narrative of immigrant odyssey had been an almost exclusively white and European one. I suspect that Obama's aura stems not just from a Tiger Woods–ishly fashionable taste for "biracialism" but from the fact that he's managed to fuse the immigrant myth of meteoric upward mobility onto the figure of a black man.

Transcending Race

Back on *Chris Matthews*, Cynthia Tucker, a black woman who writes for the *Atlanta Journal-Constitution*, responded, "He truly does seem to transcend race because his mother, after all, let's not forget, was white." Matthews agreed: "His grandmother he went to visit in Hawaii is white. Yeah." This, to me, was a baffling exchange. Obama's mother's being white is supposedly what allows him to transcend this thing called race? He looks black but he really isn't? Is blackness really only defined by Jim Crow, anger and slavery? If American-ness, at least in this equation, is defined by patronymic immigrant hope, is racial transcendence then to be defined by maternity, relation to whiteness, biology? "Transcendence" implies rising above something, cutting through, being liberated from. What would it reveal about the hidden valuations of race if one were to invert the equation by positing that Barack Obama "transcended" whiteness because his father was black?

Senator Obama has many attractive attributes—he's smart, a great writer and speaker, a skilled tactician, full of fresh vision, youthful, with a good-looking Kennedy-esque appeal. Yet there are many people to whom his appeal rests not on what he is but on what they imagine he isn't. He's not a whiner; he's not angry. He doesn't hate white people. He doesn't wear his hair like Al Sharpton. He is not the whole list of negatives that people like Chris Matthews or Joe Biden or a whole generation of f---ed-up middle-class college students identify as "blackness." Indeed, part of the reason I am anxious about the trustworthiness of Obama's widespread appeal is this unacknowledged value placed on his ability to perform "unexpected" aspects of both whiteness (as in, proud immigrant stock) and blackness (as in, his remarkable ability to discern that the sterling fish knife is not a shoe horn).

This is not just about the dualism of black and white, of course. Obama's family raised him in diverse locales—Hawaii, Indonesia, the world. Does the perception of his identity change if we think of him as our first Hawaiian presidential candidate? To paraphrase, is he the first mainstream Hawaiian-American who is articulate and bright and clean and a nice-looking guy who wouldn't be caught dead in a grass skirt holding a ukulele? Or the first mainstream Indonesian-American who is articulate and bright and clean and a nice-looking guy who had the interesting experience of going to a Roman Catholic school in a largely Muslim country, which might provide lots of useful cultural insights for a President to have in this time and place? No, unfortunately, as there are those at Fox News who can't tell a Roman Catholic school from a madrassa [Muslim school].

Worse yet, a lot of the analysis of Biden's comment has skimmed over his patronizing of Obama's substance. Rather, it has focused on whether the comments destroyed Biden's chances to run for President. Who, after all, even knew Biden had his hat in the ring?

Blackness and Authenticity

But back to Senator Obama, a presidential candidate of profound decency, extraordinary smarts and great eloquence. He was president of the *Harvard Law Review*, a position that requires not just the highest grades in the entire universe but also the unanimous acclaim of a band of viciously competitive students and a famously divided faculty. Those who make *Law Review* are immediate stars, and fabulously fast-tracked. Those who have served on the *Law Review* include a stunning and stellar array of familiar names: Supreme Court Justices Felix Frankfurter, Ruth Bader Ginsburg, Antonin Scalia, Stephen Breyer and Chief Justice John Roberts; Dean Acheson, Alger Hiss, Archibald MacLeish, Judge Richard Posner, Michael Chertoff and New York Governor Eliot Spitzer. It is, in the secretly assigned world of global power, an even better ticket to the top than being sealed in a coffin at Skull and Bones [a Yale University secret society]. It was acknowledged as such when Jews first joined the *Law Review*, when Democratic political pundit Susan Estrich became the first woman president of the *Law Review* in 1976 and when Obama became its first black president. It is a position whose credentializing power has never been questioned as far as anyone knows—at least till a few weeks ago, when the *New York Times* published an article in which Ron Klain, informal adviser to Biden's presidential bid, wondered if being president of the *Law Review* really and truly required the same skill set as being President of the United States. As a cabdriver recently expressed it to me: "Maybe the mirage in the desert is no more than a benchmark constantly being moved out of reach." (He too was articulate, and quite poetic, that cabbie. Made me wonder what benchmarks had been moved beyond *his* reach to leave him ferrying me around at midnight.)

Of course, the crown of the *Law Review* presidency is not the only aspect of Senator Obama's "authenticity" that's being refigured as a mess of thorns. If no one doubts his blackness when it comes to the uniqueness of his accomplishments while on the *Law Review*, he's apparently not "black enough" in other contexts. In another article in the *Times*, perpetual contrarians like Stanley Crouch, Debra Dickerson and Carol Swain were quoted as questioning whether he truly was a brother beneath the skin. It is surely ironic that Obama—one of the very few Americans of any stripe who has actual first-degree relatives in Africa—is being figured in some quarters as an imposter of African-American-ness.

At the same time, Obama's identity reveals the complex blindness and slipperiness of American conceptions of race, culture and ethnicity. There's a lovely quote from Saidiya Hartman's remarkable new book *Lose Your Mother*: As she wends her way through Ghana on a Fulbright Fellowship, she notes, "I was the stranger in the village, a wandering seed bereft of the possibility of taking root. Behind my back people whispered, *dua ho mmire*: a mushroom that grows on the tree has no deep soil. Everyone avoided the word 'slave,' but we all knew who was who. As a 'slave baby,' I represented what most chose to avoid: the catastrophe that was our past . . . and what was forbidden to discuss: the matter of someone's origins."

In Search of Home

As I read Hartman's words, I wondered how familiar that sentiment felt to me, or to the many African-Americans—whether they've never left our shores or traveled the world—so relentlessly in search of "home." I wondered how familiar that passage must feel to recent arrivals to our peculiarly dubbed "homeland." Just today I met a Swedish woman who is phenotypically "Asian." When she was a student at the University of California, she went to the hospital with stomach pains—and was almost committed as insane before she ever got to see a doctor, because the administrative gatekeepers simply could not reconcile her appearance with her assertion that she was a Swedish citizen.

And in this moment of unprecedented diaspora, I wonder how familiar all these sentiments must feel to Barack Obama just now. Flipped endlessly down a hall of mirrored images of blackness and whiteness, he is no less celebrated than Frederick Douglass was as one whose entire identity is mired in the exhausted exceptionalism of the "surprisingly" hyperarticulate African phenotype; yet simultaneously embraced as one who has transcended the embodiment of a troublesome past and emerged on the other side—bright as a newly minted coin, "cleansed" of baggage, of roots, of the unacknowledged rupture that is, paradoxically, our greatest national bond.

Assimilation and Jewish Ethnic Identity

Ilan Stavans

Ilan Stavans is the Lewis-Sebring professor in Latin American and Latino culture at Amherst College. In the following essay, he says that American Jews have focused on creating a map of Jewish life to the exclusion of reaching out to the rest of the world. They have shied away from multiculturalism, turned inward, and obscured the diversity within Jewish culture itself. Stavans traces the history of Jewish life in the United States, seeing how Jews assimilated and how Jewish ethnic identity has undergone shifts. He also finds that many Jewish-Americans have a stagnant perception of what it is to be Jewish and need to reinvent themselves in light of the changing racial makeup of the Jewish community in America.

A virgin world where doors of sunset part,

Saying, "Ho, all who weary, enter here!

There falls each ancient barrier that the art

of race or creed or rank devised, to rear

Grim bulwarked hatred between heart and heart!"

—*Emma Lazarus, "1492" (1889)*

Quick: name a Woody Allen movie that has a leading black actor in its cast. Time's up! Now mention a *Seinfeld* episode in which Elaine, Jerry, George, and Kramer socialize in the Upper West Side apartment with some Korean friends. How about a story about Cuban-Americans written by Isaac Bashevis Singer?

For the past several decades, American Jews have focused on creating a map of Jewish life, particularly of Jewish life as lived in Manhattan. Yet for all its realism, this map is imaginary. Artists like Allen, Seinfeld, and Singer have created a comfortably monocultural Jewish city at the expense of the multifaceted, ethnically diverse Manhattan marked by the Dominican restaurants of Washington Heights, the African-American chess players in Harlem, or the Chinese street vendors of Delancey Street.

Of course, the occasional Puerto Rican or African American character appears in these works, and there are many Jewish writers who have offered more consistently intricate multicultural pictures. Just think of the stories of Tillie Olsen and Grace Paley; the novels of E.L. Doctorow and Bernard Malamud; the poetry of Allen Ginsberg, Philip Levine, and Adrienne Rich; or the plays of Tony Kushner. But these good-will examples are exceptions to the rule. Over the past half-century, Jewish writers have generally suggested that at best they will coexist with the ethnic Other, but they will never attempt to understand these people's circumstances. They are too busy understanding themselves.

This turn inward is perplexing for many reasons. For one, it goes against the Jewish ethical imperative toward reaching out to the larger world. The inward turn also runs counter to the very basis of Jewish prosperity in America: the country's pluralism and tolerance. Think of George Washington's letter to the Hebrew Congregation of Newport, which, by stating that the U.S. government "gives to bigotry no sanction, to persecution no assistance," greased the place of Jews in America. The very multiculturalism that much recent mainstream Jewish culture has shied away from is precisely what has made Jewish life here possible.

Most of all, however, the homogenization of Jewish urban experience has obscured the diversity within the Jewish world itself.

Jewish Diversity in America

The Jewish journey in multicultural America began with the settlement in 1654 of Portuguese-speaking Sephardic Jews from Recife, Brazil, in New Amsterdam, part of the Dutch colony of New Netherland. (Ironically, of the original group of twenty-three, all but one, Asser Levy, left what would become the United States within a relatively short period of time.) Peter Stuyvesant, who served as director-general of this diverse town, wanted to keep these Jews out. He described them as "deceitful, very repugnant," and "hateful enemies and blasphemers of the name of Christ." But Jews were also seen as agents of economic growth, and Stuyvesant eventually allowed them to stay. As it turns out, this would be the onset of a community invited in initially for its mercantile talents but later embraced for its intellectual stamina.

It would systematically grow over a period of 350 years, from an original "twenty-three souls, big and small" in the French frigate named the *Ste. Catherine* to between 200 and 300 Jews in 1700, between 938,000 to 1,058,000 at the end of the nineteenth century, and between 5,340,000 and 7,700,000 at the end of the twentieth. By 1680, Ashkenazic Jews had arrived to join their Sephardic counterparts. That coexistence was never without tension as the community sought its way in the mainstream, fighting xenophobic sentiments. George Washington's revolutionary war, and the effort by the Founding Fathers, turned pluralism and tolerance into republican values that were then emphasized, with much peril, by Abraham Lincoln during and after the Civil War. Jews, Irish, Germans, and Italians mixed with the Native-American, British, and African population in what came to be known in the early part of the twentieth century as the Melting Pot, a term popularized by a British Jew, Israel Zangwill, author of *Children of the Ghetto*.

As Jews—especially the now predominant Ashkenazi Jews—worked hard to "melt" into America, they also erased their own differences. Ladino-speaking Jews, for example, as well as the Ladino media, have been all but written out of American Jewish history. We hardly ever hear about early figures in American Judaism like Haim Isaac Karigal, a visitor to the colonies from Hebron, Palestine, who in 1773 preached a sermon in the Touro Synagogue of Newport, Rhode Island, calling for loyalty, which in his view meant "obedience to the crown and denouncing public commotions and revolutions." Or Emma Lazarus, a child of a Sephardi father and German-Jewish mother, who advocated a multicultural pluralism. Or Mordecai Manuel Noah, a journalist and playwright (he is the author of *The Fortress of Sorrento* and *Natalie: or, The Frontier Maid*, among other plays) who in the first half of the nineteenth century explored the inherent tension between being an American and being Jewish.

Can Identity Be Melted?

Mordecai Manuel Noah's question about his hyphenated American-Jewish identity was prescient. As the Great Tide of Ashkenazim washed ashore, they simultaneously advocated assimilating to American values and retaining a unique Jewish identity. The tension between the one and the many, between an ethnic minority and the mainstream majority, became a staple. How to live a normalized American life, just like everyone else, and at the same time retain a sense of uniqueness? How to embrace the American values of democracy and freedom and not disappear as a millenarian people?

In the second half of the twentieth century, Jews in America seemed to have figured it all out. Just 2 percent of the population, they chose to assimilate and became increasingly influential in the worlds of moviemaking, theater, literature, music, TV, and—crucially—politics. The White House paid considerable attention to American Jewish voices. There had been prominent judicial and diplomatic figures, from Supreme Court Justice Louis D. Brandeis to Henry Kissinger, who served, for better or for worse, as representatives of the Jewish community in the larger social spectrum. This representation, obviously, would flourish in the decades to come, making Senator Joseph Lieberman the first Jew on the presidential ticket (during the Al Gore campaign in 2000) and turning the "hidden" Jewish identity of political celebrities like [Madeleine] Albright (Secretary of State during the Cinton years) and Democratic presidential hopeful John Kerry into decisive news items around the globe.

But there was another side to the coin. As Jews assimilated, the tight circle of Ashkenazic Judaism was being broken. In defining Jewish identity, the Reform and Reconstructionist movements, breaking with rabbinical tradition, have accepted patrilineal descent. Intermarriage has become accepted. Having a convert in the household, or even having non-Jews in Jewish households, is, and has been for some time, the trend. According to the National Jewish Population Survey, inter-ethnic and inter-religious marriages among American Jews at the beginning of the twenty-first century remain at a record high: between 47 percent and 51 percent. The 2000 U.S. Census Bureau stumbled in counting the number of Jews in America mainly because of the fluid ways in which Jews and non-Jews identified themselves.

Jews—ordinary Jews like my uncle and aunt—started getting worried. In the Seventies, my uncle was a successful Avenue of the Americas [a New York City street] lawyer, my aunt a devoted housewife. They had two children a bit older than me who had been raised in an assimilated milieu. But as soon as the younger of them began dating a non-Jewish girl, the parents became scared and immediately switched gears. They not only attended Reform synagogue regularly but got involved in the temple's board. Soon they were emphasizing their Jewishness in a way I had never seen before. By the time their daughter-in-law married into the family, she had undergone a conversion: not only did she embrace Judaism as a religion but, lo and behold, domestically she became the center of attention. Soon the newlyweds moved to his parents' home, arguably in order to keep the family together.

This story reflects concerns many Jews have begun to feel. As Jews solidify their status at the center of the Melting Pot, inner doubts have emerged about the road the community has taken in order to become fully American. Have we given up too much of our ethnic identity? Is complete assimilation the sole way into a full American identity, as it was thought in the Fifties?

"Re-Ethnification"

Even as assimilated Jews began to ask these questions, the ethnic identity of Jews in the United States was undergoing another profound shift. Just as the Ashkenazim had washed ashore in the late nineteenth century, a new tide of immigrant Jews has been steadily making America its home at the start of the twenty-first. As a result of political instability and the collapse of Third-World economies, Jews from south of the Rio Grande—from Cuba, Argentina, Brazil, Mexico, Panama, and Peru—have moved north in search of freedom and happiness. Likewise Jews from Russia and the former Soviet bloc, as well as those from countries like South Africa, Syria, Iran, and Egypt: tired of the anti-Semitism in their countries of origin and eager to grant their children a fair education, they have relocated to the major centers of Jewish life in America. Since its inception in 1948, Israel has also been a magnet for Jews from around the globe. But the political impasse in the Middle East has unquestionably made *aliyah* [the immigration of Jews to Israel] unattractive to thousands, who have redirected themselves to the "blessed land" of New York and Los Angeles. As a result of these new immigrants, the monoculture of Ashkenazim is under assault.

Between Ashkenazic fears of intermarriage and the growing multiethnic identity of American Jews, the old dream of full and unequivocal assimilation once embraced by Ashkenazic Jews is now drastically being reversed. Young American Jews are, as ever, proud to stress the *American* half of their identity. But they are less unequivocal about losing their ethnic identity than their forebears had been. Indeed, their objective, I believe, is to be *hyphenated* Jews, ethnic creatures loyal to their minority background without sacrificing their patriotism.

All this, in my view, amounts to a thorough process of what I would call "re-ethnification," a collective recognition by American Jews not only of their Jewishness as a form of ethnicity but also of the fact that to be Jewish in the United States one doesn't need to trace one's roots to Central and Eastern Europe. American Jews come from everywhere. There can be African-American Jews, Asian Jews, Native-American Jews, and Latino Jews, as well as what the U.S. Census Bureau has defined as "other," not to mention, obviously, Sephardic and Mizrahi. In other words, while intermarriage drives Ashkenazim to re-ethnicize so that they remain Jewish, Jews of other ethnicities embrace ethnification in order to maintain an identity apart from the Ashkenazim. In short, to be a Jew and an American one must be aware of one's own hyphenated nature.

This "re-ethnification" process is of dramatic relevance. It isn't about purity at either end of the hyphen. Instead, it is about cross-fertilization on all sides, a process that not only allows Jews and non-Jews to find a middle ground but also has initiated within the Jewish community a move to energize the center by pointing to different places of the Diaspora, not just to Eastern Europe and Israel.

Multiculturalism

Multiculturalism has been a feature of the United States since its inception, but as the population numbers have changed, so has the texture of society and its principles. It used to be that new immigrants would eventually be allowed a space within the mainstream culture. But multiculturalism has finally changed the mainstream: it subverted and decentralized it. Already 12 percent of the nation's entire population is non-U.S. born. And by the mid-twenty-first century only one American in four will be of European descent.

In an increasingly heterogeneous America, Jews will have to establish bridges and make alliances with groups of non-European origin, whose idiosyncrasies, it might be assumed, are likely to require a different kind of cultural sensibility. In recounting Jewish history in general, American Jews seldom stress the period of *La Convivencia* in the Iberian Peninsula prior to the expulsion. Now that Latinos in the United States are fundamental players on the social chessboard, are Jews familiar enough with the Hispanic psyche and history to create a partnership with the various Latino subgroups, such as Mexican-Americans, Cuban-Americans, Dominican-Americans, and Puerto Ricans on the mainland? Will we be willing to bring back the history of our own Sephardi communities in order to find common ground with our fellow citizens?

Since the Enlightenment [Eighteenth century], Jews have served as agents of modernization. They have helped make America competitive at almost every level. But Jewish cultural perception has become stagnant. To the question "Who are we?" a majority of American Jews, I believe more by inertia than anything else, still respond as they did after World War II, pointing to Europe as the source of cultural and religious sustenance. But we are no longer primarily European Jews, nor is America primarily a country that looks to Europe. A major demographic metamorphosis has taken place, one that gives room to the less monolithic, more varied nation we live in. Throughout history, Jews have strived to reinvent themselves in diversity. Think of Woody Allen's *Zelig* as a paradigm. But that multicultural self is still not recognized as a communal feature. It needs to become one if we are likely to identify as our own the face in the mirror.

CHAPTER 2

Race, Ethnicity, and the New American Landscape

Immigration and Intolerance in America's Heartland

Stephen G. Bloom

Stephen G. Bloom teaches journalism at the University of Iowa. In the following essay, he shows how immigration, much of it illegal, is changing the face of rural America. Bloom sees the new immigrants to small towns as pioneers solidly in the American pioneering tradition. They come to Iowa's slaughterhouse boomtowns, casinos, and revivalist communities seeking opportunity in the form of low-paying, menial jobs locals refuse to take. He focuses on Iowa's meat-packing industry, where a recent wave of illegal Mexican and Central American pioneers has replaced a 1990s wave of Hasidic immigrants from eastern and central Europe in the kosher slaughterhouse in Postville, straining the town's educational system and social fabric. Bloom notes that wages in meat production have dropped from $19 per hour plus benefits in 1980 to $6.25 per hour with few or no benefits. While only some of these pioneers stay—many return home after a few months, never to return, and others come and go as itinerant workers—their numbers, combined with the exodus of educated young people, mean that rural America is becoming an increasingly heterogeneous place.

Four states—California, Texas, New York, and Florida—get two-thirds of the nation's immigrants. But for many immigrants these states serve only as ports of entry; once inside the United States they move north, east, and west, converging in rural America in waves of secondary migration. Other newcomers head directly inland, altogether bypassing coastal cities. However the immigrants get here, rural America, which

Stephen G. Bloom, "The New Pioneers," *The Wilson Quarterly*, summer 2006, pp. 60–68. Reproduced by permission of the publisher and the author.

makes up 75 percent of the landmass of the United States, is up for grabs as tens of thousands of pioneers, almost all Hispanic, arrive each month.

While the countryside is changing fast, these newcomers arrive in a place where homes still sell for $40,000, a serious crime is toilet-papering a high schooler's front yard, the only smog comes from a late-autumn bonfire, and getting stuck in traffic means being trapped behind a John Deere tractor on Main Street. But immigrants don't flock here for the quality of life. They come for one reason: jobs. They are taking the places of the old who are dying, the young who are leaving, and the locals who refuse to take the low-paying, menial jobs that abound. In doing so, they are shaping rural America's future. . . .

At the University of Iowa, where I teach, 60 percent of graduates each year choose to leave the state. With diplomas in hand, few want much to do with farming or living in a state where the nearest movie theater might be a 30-mile drive and the first freestanding Starbucks store opened [in 2004]. From 1980 to 1990, all but seven of Iowa's 99 counties lost population. School districts consolidated or closed. If any state needed an influx of new residents, it was Iowa.

Immigrants Work for Low Pay

And that's what it got, starting in the mid-1990s. Almost all the newcomers were Hispanic immigrants, some legal, most illegal. Between 1990 and 2000 Iowa's population grew by 5.4 percent, to 2.9 million. Two-thirds of that growth was due to immigrants, mostly Latinos and mostly from Mexico. By 2000, Iowa's Hispanic population had grown 153 percent. The 2000 census counted 82,500 Hispanics in Iowa, but many say today that there are upwards of 150,000 here. By 2030, half of Iowa's population of three million is expected to belong to minority groups. By far the greatest number will be Hispanics working in low-level jobs.

Entry-level work for these newcomers is plentiful, usually as kill-floor employees at slaughterhouses, where workers don't need to know a word of English. The only requirements are a strong stomach and a strong back. It's no wonder locals spurn dangerous work as knockers, stickers, bleeders, tail rippers, flankers, gutters, sawers, and plate boners, toiling on what amounts to a "disassembly line." Turnover in these grueling jobs often exceeds 100 percent annually. Safety instruction is minimal, particularly at many rural meatpacking houses, and the high turnover results in a revolving work force of inexperienced employees prone to accidents.

The journey to this jobs mecca is not without its own perils. Many Americans got a glimpse of those dangers in October 2002, when 11 smuggled Mexican immigrants were found dead inside a sealed Union Pacific grain hopper railcar in the Iowa meatpacking town of Denison, 130 miles west of Des Moines, that had originated in the border city of Matamoros, Mexico. . . .

Once immigrants arrive, securing work is relatively easy. Just showing up at the employment window with a Social Security card, which can be purchased for as little as $100, is usually all that's required. So many undocumented immigrants have converged on rural slaughterhouses that, even if there were a mandate to enforce employment laws, the immigration authorities couldn't begin to do so. The dirty secret in rural states about undocumented workers is that, politicians' and industry leaders' comments to the contrary, it is very much in their best interest to keep things the way they are. Without undocumented workers, the U.S. meat-processing industry would grind to a halt.

For more than a century, slaughterhouses were located in cities. Chicago rose to prominence because of its famed cattle-processing industry. The city's Union Stock Yards opened in 1865 and eventually grew to 475 acres of slaughterhouses. Today, only one slaughterhouse remains in Chicago. Industry leaders realized decades ago that it made more economic sense to bring meatpacking plants to corn-fed livestock than to truck livestock to far-off slaughterhouses in expensive cities with strong unions. Refrigeration allowed for processed meat to be trucked without spoilage. At the same time, the industry became highly mechanized. Innovations such as air- and electric-powered knives made skilled butchers unnecessary. Larger plants in rural outposts became more profitable than small urban slaughterhouses.

Wages for union meat-production workers peaked in 1980 at $19 an hour, not including benefits. Today at many slaughterhouses, located in isolated pockets of America, starting pay is often not much more than minimum wage, with few or no benefits. At Postville's meatpacking plant, pay starts at $6.25 an hour. Health insurance is available to workers and their families at about $50 a week, but few can afford such a hefty deduction, and many immigrant workers aren't familiar with the concept of health insurance plans. Some don't believe they'll need the coverage, some think there must be a catch to it, and some figure they'll be fired or deported if injured. . . .

Variety of Work for Immigrants

Much has been written about the proliferation of fast-food restaurants and Wal-Mart stores in the rural United States, where, if immigrants can procure documents, they often find work. But little has been noted about another industry that increasingly serves as a job magnet for newcomers: legalized casino gambling, with its insatiable appetite for low-wage restaurant and service workers, laborers, maids, and janitors. . . . The casino industry makes peculiarly efficient use of the immigrant work force, targeting non-English-speakers as both low-wage workers and gamblers, in a new spin on the old company store. Immigrant workers return much of their wages by gambling in the same casinos that employ them. When all four new Iowa casinos are in operation, they will employ as many as 2,000 low-income workers, and that doesn't include those in building trades needed to construct these gambling palaces. . . .

Some newly arrived immigrants do what they can to integrate with their rural neighbors and start the process of becoming Americanized; most, though, do not. There's no need to try to fit in. In Marshalltown, Iowa, for example, one-quarter of the slaughterhouse production employees, about 450, come from the Mexican town of Villachuato in the state of Michoacán. These workers, mostly men, travel frequently between Villachuato and Marshalltown, but few become permanent residents of Iowa. In a sense, they are commuters—working to earn money in Iowa, saving and sending it back home to Mexico, then returning to their families for months at a time. While here, they live and work together, forming a tight-knit Mexican enclave.

Postville, Iowa, has become a classic boomtown. In 1986, Aaron Rubashkin, a Hasidic butcher from Brooklyn, New York, bought a defunct slaughterhouse in Postville, installed his sons as managers, and soon started killing the rich, corn-fed Iowa beef. The meatpacking plant, AgriProcessors, ultimately became the largest kosher slaughterhouse in the world. As more and more Hasidim moved to town, tiny Postville became home to the most rabbis per capita of any municipality outside Jerusalem (meat must be certified by a rabbi to be labeled kosher). Hasidic Jews belong to one of 40 or so ultra-Orthodox sects; Rubashkin, his sons, and many who settled in Postville are members of one of the largest, Lubavitch. The kosher slaughterhouse in Postville operates six days a week, except for the Jewish Sabbath and holidays, and has a seemingly never-ending need to fill its 800 jobs. As many as 90 percent of its workers are Hispanic. In 1990, the town's population was stagnant at 1,472. By 2000, Postville had grown 64 percent, to 2,273, and today its population is 2,352. Unofficial estimates place the population closer to 2,600, about one-quarter Hispanic.

When I started reporting on Postville in the mid-1990s, the kosher slaughterhouse owners flatly told me they preferred to hire Eastern Europeans over Hispanics. Most workers on the kill floor then were neither Jews nor locals, but Russians, Ukrainians, Kazakhs, Bosnians, and Poles. . . .

Today, Eastern Europeans by and large have stopped coming to Postville. The slaughterhouse jobs are too menial and the pay too low. Most of these workers have begun the process of mainstreaming into larger cities in the state—Des Moines, Cedar Rapids, Dubuque. At Spice-N-Ice, the vodka has given way to Mexican beers and tequilas, but the store's owner says most Mexicans he sees prefer American products such as Budweiser beer and Black Velvet whiskey. . . .

New Wave of Immigrants

Like many onetime immigrant communities, from New York's Lower East Side to Los Angeles' Boyle Heights, the areas of Postville that once belonged to locals, and later to Eastern Europeans, now have given way to Latino immigrants. Newcomers who don't live in trailers or storefront apartments in town find their way to a complex of newly built but already deteriorating duplexes and apartment buildings north of town. At least 225 workers—about a third Guatemalans and two-thirds Mexicans—live in the complex. A sparsely furnished two-bedroom apartment rents for about $400 a month, says one of the landlords, Kermit Miller. A Pentecostal church is scheduled to be built within the complex in the next six months. (About half of Postville's Guatemalans are Pentecostals, who for now meet in the basement of the Presbyterian church for services.)

Many Hispanics gather at the two Mexican restaurants in town, Sabor Latino and Red Rooster (which serves Tex-Mex food). On Saturdays, when AgriProcessors shuts down, the coin-operated Laundromat in town, Family Laundry, is a busy place. There's also a new Mexican clothing store, El Vaquero (the Cowboy), which sells sombreros, Mexican-style baby clothes and dresses (particularly for baptisms and *quinceañeras* [girls' fifteenth-birthday celebrations]), shirts, and Mexican flags. Every night, scores of Mexican men play soccer in an open field at the edge of town.

Attempts to Americanize Hispanic immigrants generally begin in school programs designed to teach English to children of workers who do bring their families. This approach has produced mixed results. In Postville, the influx of immigrants has spurred a white flight of Anglo students to outlying school districts. Superintendent David Strudthoff doesn't mince words when he says white parents who pull their children out of the school district are engaging in "ethnic cleansing." To prevent the student body's ethnic makeup from becoming more lopsided, Postville created a desegregation plan in 2003 that allows two Anglo students to transfer out of the district only if one new immigrant student matriculates.

Cost of Education

Immigration is a double-edged sword in small towns such as Postville. This fall, the Postville Community School District will receive $5,141 per year per Anglo student, which comes from property taxes and state education coffers. But for each immigrant student, the state will chip in an additional appropriation that goes toward hiring teachers to provide English-language instruction, bringing the total to $6,272. For Hasidic families in Postville who send their children to the yeshiva [Jewish school] in town, the school district will realize $3,084 per student. More than a third of the 578 students currently enrolled in Postville's public schools are immigrant children. The proportion of immigrants is 14 percent in high school and 29 percent in middle school. In the town's elementary school, it jumps to 55 percent.

In an era when rural schools are consolidating because of dwindling enrollments, Postville school numbers are strong.

Since 1999 the district has received grants of more than $2 million from government agencies earmarked for a variety of purposes, but, says Strudthoff, all are based on the increased number of immigrant children attending Postville schools. The latest grant requires a dual-track language program. Starting in the fall, all Postville kindergarten students will receive mandatory half-day immersion instruction in both Spanish and English, and Spanish-language training will be required for all students in each subsequent grade level through high school.

Changing Religious Communities

For the most part, rural American towns have always been self-contained extended families, with just about every resident white and Christian. For many Iowans, shared faith is the litmus test for acceptance. Since many Hispanic immigrants are Catholic, religion is one area where relatively little assimilation would appear necessary. Most natives in this part of Iowa are Lutherans, but many towns have a Catholic church as well. In part to attract this younger, emerging constituency, several years ago the priest at St. Bridget's Church, Paul Ouderkirk, decided to celebrate Mass once a week in Spanish.

More than a few local parishioners retaliated by taking their prayers 10 miles down Highway 18 to St. Patrick's Church in Monona, where Mass is strictly an English-language affair. "A small group told me that the migrants were stealing our Mass," Father Ouderkirk told me recently. "They said their ancestors built the church, and because of that, they deserved all Masses to be in their language." Another group of Anglo parishioners took a different tack, said Ouderkirk. "They said that if I continued with Mass in Spanish, I'd be catering to the Hispanics, and they'd never move away." Ouderkirk is now retired, but he returns to Postville to celebrate one Spanish Mass a week.

A Change in Community

Postville is still the kind of community where parents drop their kids off at the municipal pool on Wilson Street to swim all day long without worry. Everyone's phone number still starts with the same 864 prefix. But the insulated nature of the town is changing. Residents lock their doors now—both front and back. Crime isn't rampant, but it's more common than it was 10 years ago, when on a summer night residents would leave their car engines running while they popped into Casey's convenience store on Tilden for a cherry ICEE.

A large number of single Hispanic men in their twenties live in Postville with little to do but work, sleep, and hang out. As in other meatpacking communities, few have high school educations. They belong to the demographic group with the highest incidence of criminal activities, write rural anthropologists Michael J. Broadway and Donald D. Stull.

Since 2000, there have been one murder and three attempted murders involving Postville immigrants. Drugs are a reminder of the influx of newcomers. Authorities suspect that the Mississippi River town of Prairie Du Chien, 26 miles away is a hub for drug trafficking. In June [2006], Postville police and the Clayton County sheriff's office were instrumental in a bust in Rockford, Illinois, that yielded 625 pounds of marijuana. Drunk-driving arrests in Postville went from two in 1992 to 36 last year. Domestic trouble calls to the police in 1992 totaled 32; last year there were triple that number.

In every community, cultural norms are tested when newcomers arrive. When five local high school boys gather on a Postville street corner on a Saturday night and wave at a local girl driving her dad's pickup, that's OK. In fact, it's what everyone expects. But when five Hispanic guys on a corner whistle at the same girl? This can stretch community tolerance, leading to talk of Hispanic gangs, not to mention the endangered virginity of heartland daughters.

Politicians have exploited such fears with varying degrees of success. Steve King, a Republican congressman from the western quadrant of the state, blames immigrants for many of Iowa's ills, employing some fairly vitriolic rhetoric. "Thousands of Americans die at the hands of illegal aliens every year," one of King's press releases reads. "Every murder, every rape, every violent gang crime committed against Americans by illegal aliens is an utterly preventable crime." King is riding a crest of conservative anti-immigrant support in Iowa. A bill now pending in the Iowa legislature would prevent banks from awarding home mortgages to illegal immigrants. The state supreme court ruled in 2005 that undocumented persons are not eligible for driver's licenses. The net impact is that many undocumented workers drive illegally, with no insurance.

In Postville, some members of the city council appear frustrated by the indelible impact of newcomers. First the Hasidim came to town and reopened the long-defunct slaughterhouse and made it hum, and now Hispanics have converged on Postville to work there. In May, the *Postville Herald-Leader* published this council member:

> A diversity of values is at the core of what some want to call racist or bigots or anti-Semite. One group wants to isolate itself, by dressing a little differently, keeping their children out of our public schools and wanting a different day for the Sabbath. They generally will not eat in other establishments. Another group here sends money back to other foreign countries and brings with it a lack of respect for our laws and culture which contribute to unwed mothers, trash in the streets, unpaid bills, drugs, forgery, and other crimes. We also have savvy employers that hire people at the lowest possible rates to obtain the greatest value to their company, which in turn contributes to overcrowded housing and increased use of public services and lowers the standard of living.

People Find Opportunity

Unless something wholly unexpected happens, more and more immigrants will stream into rural America. Some will return home after a few months and never come back; others will be itinerant workers, coming and going, in constant flux; many will stay and become part of the evolving social fabric of the rural United States. A separate group, already Americanized, will not arrive directly from their homelands, but from crowded coastal cities, seeking middle-class opportunities—buying up property and starting businesses. Other newcomers, like the Hasidim in Postville, will be members of cohesive religious groups that move to rural America because of affordable land and a longing for isolation.

"Pioneers go places civilized people shun," writes Iowa historian Michael J. Bell. "And they tend to go there, wherever 'there' is, because the one thing they can be sure of is that civilization is not there waiting to tell them how things ought to be done." That's why disciples of the Maharishi Mahesh Yogi incorporated a community in 2001 near Fairfield, Iowa, 200 miles south of Postville, and called it Vedic City, where more than 150 homes, topped with small gold-colored vessels, face east, and community-wide, meditation sessions take place twice a day. It's why more than 125 families belonging to a cult called the Old Believers—which in dress and custom attempts to mimic life in 17th-century Russia—settled in rural Erskine, Minnesota, in 1998. And it's why Mennonites have moved into the north-central Iowa town of Riceville, buying up local businesses and starting their own school.

The common thread running through slaughterhouse boomtowns, casino outposts, and revivalist communities is opportunity—whether rooted in economics or in faith. The stories of these small towns are parables of change in rural America, where unplanned and uncontrolled social experiments are taking place. This aging, long-neglected region is being defined anew by a pioneer mentality sustained by young blood and vitality. Power is seldom relinquished easily, and many of these rural towns are, or will be, battlegrounds for acrimonious power struggles.

People in rural America have gotten along just fine for more than 150 years. But times have changed. The only way the natives of these insular communities will gain traction as their own numbers continue to dwindle is to forge power alliances with newcomers. How successfully thousands of rural towns enfold newcomers into a workable social structure foreshadows how the greater American society will be able to incorporate larger and larger blocs of new Americans who increasingly demand to be defined on their own terms.

Immigrants by nature are pioneers—as American as Huck Finn [in Mark Twain's book], who reckoned he had "to light out for the Territory ahead of the rest." That's what immigrants do. A sense of purpose and adventure pushes them to seek their futures in unfamiliar and distant places, while others back home, perhaps more timid, choose to stay put. It is in getting to such faraway places, often in tiny rural towns, and staking their claim, that these new pioneers are forever changing the rules of America—and of becoming American.

Asian Americans in the Twenty-First Century

James Kyung-Jin Lee is a professor at the University of California, Santa Barbara, in the Department of Asian American Studies. At the time the following essay was written, he was professor of English and Asian American studies and associate director for the Center for Asian American Studies at the University of Texas, Austin. In the essay, he discusses the creation of the term Asian American *by Yuji Ichioka in the 1960s and goes on to describe the success of Asian Americans and their increasing intellectual and cultural visibility in the decades that followed. He considers what has accounted for the transformation of Asians from "national menace" to "model minority" and considers the new complexities this has brought for the culture.*

As the rest of the nation, and indeed the world, prepared to commemorate the one-year anniversary of the September 11 [2001] terrorist attacks, a quieter remembrance was taking place in the halls of Asian American Studies programs around the United States. There was a special kind of grief at UCLA's [University of California, Los Angeles] Asian American Studies Center on September 6, 2002, when director Don T. Nakanishi issued a press release announcing the death of Yuji Ichioka on September 1. For more than three decades, Ichioka held the position of Senior Researcher at the Center; he taught the Center's first class shortly after its establishment in 1969. An award-winning author, he was effectively the creator of Asian America in the sense that, in 1968, while a young graduate student at the University of California at Berkeley, he coined the term "Asian American," and helped found the anti-

James Kyung-Jin Lee, *The Cambridge Companion to Modern American Culture.* New York: Cambridge University Press, 2006. Copyright © 2006 Cambridge University Press. Reprinted with the permission of Cambridge University Press.

Vietnam war, antiracist student group, the Asian American Political Alliance. The Asian students at San Francisco State College, who along with black, Chicana/o, Native, and leftist white students shut down the school for five months in a historic strike to call for, among many things, the establishment of a School of Ethnic Studies, might opt to identify themselves more as part of the "Third World Liberation Front" than a self-identified racial group, but gradually "Asian American" became the accepted descriptive term.

1968, the year of the "days of rage" in Todd Gitlin's formulation, was pivotal in the development of US cultural politics and political culture. For Gitlin, it marked the beginning of the end of the New Left and its "years of hope," as groups such as Students for a Democratic Society (SDS) degenerated into the ultra-radical Weathermen; likewise, the southern-based civil rights movements led by avowedly nonviolent and mostly Christian-led groups, began to lose legitimacy to Black Power, particularly in poor, urban neighborhoods. Two years earlier, [Stokely] Carmichael replaced John Lewis as the head of the Student Nonviolent Coordinating Committee (SNCC), belying its name and effectively making armed resistance an option for the group in its struggle against white supremacy. But whereas Gitlin casts aspersions on the rise of this new militancy, others celebrate 1968 as a watershed moment in the development of historical self-consciousness among non-white peoples living in the United States, of which Asian Americans would be a part. While most historians of this period regard the rise of radicalism as a major reason why the general US public shifted concretely and perhaps inexorably to the political Right, evidenced by [President Richard] Nixon's decisive victory for the "silent majority," the so-called "death" of the New Left took place coterminously with the birth of, among other things, "Asian America," created, debated, and nurtured in classrooms, activist meetings, social service agencies, poetry gatherings, and of course anti-Vietnam war rallies.

Defining a Group

That Ichioka developed the term "Asian American" in the midst of protest against the United States' involvement in Vietnam throughout the 1960s is not simply historical coincidence. Something new was happening in the political air late in this decade that demanded new names, new formations, new values. One could argue that opposition to the war hit closer to home for Asian Americans than for other Americans; after all, this was a war fought in an Asian country, in fact one of the poorest, and as many Asian American soldiers returning from Vietnam later testified, it was like a brother fighting a brother. Still, since the turn of the twentieth century, the United States has intervened militarily in Asia on at least three other occasions before Vietnam: the Philippine-American War that followed the United States' conflict with Spain, World War II with the United States fighting Japan in the aftermath of the Pearl Harbor attacks, and the US defense of South Korea against so-called communist "aggression" from the North. In contrast to the 1960s, there were neither mass protests against US military involvement in Asia nor organized resistance to the war effort as would be the case with respect to Vietnam. People of Asian descent living in the United States did not share political convictions, let alone a sense of common interest, during these earlier international conflicts. Vietnam brought together former ethnic antagonists and while this coalition was never an easy one, it was a signal event not least because throughout the twentieth century one could otherwise offer little evidence of such panethnic solidarity.

The key to understanding the development of Asian America in 1968 is the conference at Bandung in 1955. When world leaders of newly decolonized nations from Africa and Asia gathered in Indonesia to further the strategy of "nonalignment" in the context of the US and Soviet scramble for world influence, they evidenced and prompted a sense of shared purpose, even if this solidarity was not always adhered to. Yet if the twenty-nine nations represented at Bandung would eventually fall victim to a de facto dependence on the former colonial powers (neo-colonialism), the official push to decolonization propelled by the chaos of World War II simultaneously brought new hopes for an expansion of social and political freedom as well as new anxieties and vulnerabilities. Bandung in 1955 led directly to the Non-aligned Movement of 1961, still in existence today. Despite the fact that China's invasion of India dashed any hope of the "Third World" forming a significant bloc against, in particular, western capitalist encroachment, the visual representation of non-white peoples joining together was as indelible as the tragedy of the political ineffectiveness of this movement for the next half-century. . . .

A Model Minority

Two feature stories—one published in January [1966] in the *New York Times* and entitled "Success Story: Japanese-American Style," the other printed in December of the same year in *U.S. News and World Report*, called "Success Story of One Minority Group in the US" about Chinese Americans— proffered a new image of Asian Americans, who, in overcoming bitter racial discrimination, displayed social practices worthy of general American praise. Asian Americans, these articles suggested, with their low crime rates, high educational attainment, and, most importantly, little need for governmental welfare programs, were emerging as "model minorities," in stark contrast to the claims of racial injury and the need for state action from other communities of color. In fact, the second story on Chinese Americans makes the comparison explicit: "At a time when it is being proposed that hundreds of billions of dollars be spent to uplift Negroes and other minorities, the nation's 300,000 Chinese Americans are moving ahead on their own, with no help from anyone else." A barely concealed swipe at President [Lyndon] Johnson's "War on Poverty," the biggest expansion of social welfare since the New

Deal, and a more muted attack on the growing influence of the Black Power movement, these articles set up a coherent political and social trajectory for Asian Americans. This definitively aligned Asian Americans with the dominant social order, in contrast to the forces of rebellion and reform, and offered them a claim to full citizenship with the proviso that they disavow any kinship with the "other minorities."

It is this transformation of the Asian from national menace to ideal model that characterizes the ambivalent story of Asian Americans in the twentieth century. The "model minority" has re-emerged in the 1980s and 1990s, revised to appeal to an idea of multiculturalism that is no less damning of poor, "undeserving" blacks, especially in the wake of the Los Angeles uprisings of 1992, which will forever be visualized as a conflict between Korean storeowners "defending" their property and black and brown looters. Asian American parents in San Francisco and some public figures have used the educational success of wealthy Asian American (and some educationally exceptional and materially poor) students to attack affirmative action and other redistributive programs in public services. In the twenty-first century, and particularly in the aftermath of the September 11 events in 2001, this Asian American neoconservatism has moved beyond domestic policy and into international affairs. Men such as Viet Dinh, former Assistant Attorney General of President George W. Bush's administration, helped coauthor the Patriot Act, a law that granted governmental agencies broad power to investigate, survey, and detain without due process. On the west coast, University of California law professor John Yoo has made the case that in the realm of international law in the age of terrorism, the United States is not subject to the United Nations–ratified Geneva Conventions. To this extent, Yoo asserts, there are cases in which torture can be legally sanctioned as a legitimate tool in the United States' war arsenal, and the indefinite detention of prisoners, now dubbed enemy combatants, upheld. The alignment of Asian American neoconservatives to the rightist drift in US political culture in the last two decades has won a substantial, if not universal, following within Asian American communities. Vietnamese Americans, for example, whose mostly refugee population suffered first hand the war that brought other Asian Americans to mass protest in the 1960s, are overwhelmingly supportive of conservative Republican candidates, the effects of the perceived correspondence between conservatism and anti-communism.

Indeed, as some have suggested that the increasing Asian American presence in intellectual and popular culture will actually transform what it means to be "white" in twenty-first century America, the forces of capitalist globalization and the attendant transnationalism of both goods and people put greater pressure on the term Asian "American." Intellectuals from the Indian subcontinent have engaged in vigorous debate amongst themselves and with other Asian American scholars and, armed with the powerful discourse of postcolonial theory, have turned to questions of diaspora and collective nostalgia as critical categories through which to explore community formation. The emergence of South Asian American Studies has brought newfound attention to the complexity of Asian American belonging: for even as the South Asian presence has a century-long history since the arrival of mostly Punjabi Sikhs in California, this historiography has been largely and perhaps necessarily "forgotten" by more recent, professional, and wealthy South Asians from the post-1965 era. Correspondingly, there are some communities categorized by the US Census Bureau as Asian American that remain virtually unorganized and out of mainstream sight except when criminalized: Cambodian Americans, for example, suffer unemployment rates in places like Long Beach, California, as high as 40 percent, and make their way into American consciousness through their popular demonization as gang members. In Hawaii, the myth of multiculturalism that has pervaded the islands because of its Asian majority has been dispelled by calls from Native Hawaiians who argue that "Asian Americans" constitute nothing less than the latest wave of colonial settlers to impose their power on the sovereign rights of its indigenous peoples.

At a moment when Asian Americans have enjoyed visibility in ways unimaginable earlier in the twentieth century—cultural, social, economic—the political foundations that underwrote the term in 1968 have, then, been put into significant crisis. No longer, for example, are Asian American writers merely "ethnic" representatives; indeed, among the current crop of highly-touted *American* writers a significant number are of Asian descent. Chang-rae Lee's protagonist in the author's debut novel, *Native Speaker* (1995), does nor suffer alienation from American culture, but rather struggles because his English is *too* perfect, his capacity to understand the nuances of America's contradictions too easy to coopt. Henry, Lee's narrator, is a self-conscious "model minority," a far cry from the Asian American figure Ichioka imagined in 1968, but in gaining a kind of aptitude that allows him safe travel across the social spectrum in New York City, Henry loses the language that is at once the privilege and cost of assimilation: "My ugly immigrant's truth ... is that I have exploited my own, and those others who can be exploited. . . . Here is all of my American education."

Disparity of Class

For those who have enjoyed the social rewards that stemmed from the post-1965 transformations in the United States, it has never been easier to "belong," but the imperative remains. Jhumpa Lahiri's protagonist, in the final story of her Pulitzer Prize–winning *The Interpreter of Maladies* (1999), meditates on his life of immigration and settlement, from Bengal to Boston via London. The sheer ordinariness of his experience becomes itself an epic tale of continents coming together:

"there are times when it is beyond my imagination." Also beyond his imagination, however, perhaps necessarily so, are those working-class Bengalis he must leave behind in London. Combine this specific literary forgetting with the larger contemporary class stratification of many Asian American communities—the extremely poor at one end and the very wealthy at the other—and much remains beyond the imagination of these newly minted Asian American paragons of American culture. It is perhaps for this reason that [author] Vijay Prashad cleverly asks of Asian Americans, in a rhetorical reversal of [African American writer and educator] W. E. B. DuBois's query: "How does it feel to be a solution?" The answer, of course, is not simple at all; there is, after all, complexity in complicity. So long branded America's "problem," it is thus not surprising that a willful forgetfulness by Asian Americans offers provisional, even if fraught, satisfaction.

While complicity and crisis have generated new complexities for Asian American culture, however, making definitions elusive, even impossible, the term continues to generate new meanings. Never before have so many Asian Americans pieced together the differential histories with other communities of color both through popular culture and in direct political action. Korean American activists in Los Angeles have attacked the exploitation of mostly Mexican and Central American workers by Korean-owned businesses, and have waged a decade-long campaign to advocate workers' rights. Earlier in the 1970s and 1980s, Japanese Americans rejected municipal plans to redevelop downtown areas by inviting Japanese corporate capital, in effect turning working-class residential neighborhoods into spaces attractive to out-of-town commerce and tourism, and tried to envision what a "Japanese American" community as an interracial space might mean.

Cross-racial imaginations challenge and transform what it means to be Asian American. South Asian Americans "remix" hip-hop-infused bhangra dance parties into what one scholar has referred to as a "queer diaspora," transforming older internationalisms into a new, if unlikely, form of solidarity. These alternative formations, at the very least, stand in clear contrast to the seemingly inexorable march of Asian Americans into the domain of neoconservative "whiteness." Indeed, within the short history of Asian American complicity, and complexity, there remains an Asian American culture, perhaps nothing more than a subcultural presence, which keeps alive the conviction that stirred Yuji Ichioka to think of calling himself something new and different.

Attitudes Toward Muslims After September 11

Behzad Yaghmaian

Behzad Yaghmaian is an Iranian-born American citizen and a professor at Ramapo College in New Jersey. In the following essay, he considers the unknown victims of September 11—the Muslim immigrants who are now considered potential terrorists by dint of their religion and ethnicity. He describes his interrogation by a police officer at the U.S. border, which brings flashbacks of his maltreatment by the Islamic Republic in Iran and a feeling of homelessness in the United States. He describes the stories of Muslim immigrants who have suffered mistreatment and how racial profiling and suspicion has become a routine facet of their lives.

It was a beautiful and sunny day that September 11th and I was in New York's Central Park biking when I saw the helicopters flying south. Sirens and more helicopters followed. Sensing that something troubling had happened, I headed for home.

On my way into my building, I was stopped by a harmless, mentally-impaired man, a street regular in our neighborhood. With a frantic look, he stuttered out, "Did you hear? The Arabs have attacked!" Then he said it again. "The Arabs" was what I heard as I headed for my apartment, hoping he was wrong. What could he know? I thought, only half-convinced.

By midday, of course, everyone was talking about the Muslims, the Arabs, the Middle Eastern terrorists. I remained in my room, avoiding suspicious neighborhood eyes, watching the Twin Towers crumble again and again on screen. I had lived in the United States for years, but already I feared I had somehow become an outsider—a suspected outsider. I feared the start of a witch-hunt against people who looked like me. Some of my American friends, who had the same fears, called offering, for instance, to drive me to work the next day. "Nobody will bother you if you're with me," said one. "Stay here with us and you won't have to drive at all," said another who lived near the college where I taught economics.

Muslims as Potential Terrorists

Long before September 11, I had decided to write a book about the journey of millions of desperate migrants seeking in the West a life free of violence and poverty. The attacks of September 11th narrowed my focus to Muslim migrants who were now regarded as potential terrorists and a threat to national security. As the months passed and the President's "war on terror" began, I prepared for a long eastward journey of my own in order to follow Muslim migrants west in search of new homes. Expecting to be away for at least two years, I visited Quebec in May 2002 to say farewell to friends.

Early on a Saturday morning, bidding my friends in Quebec goodbye, I drove towards the U.S. border less than an hour away. Lining up behind the other cars, I reached over and unzipped the side pocket of my knapsack, got my American passport out, checked all my documents, and slowly approached passport control. A middle-aged woman with short blond hair and a blank face took my passport.

"Where are you going, sir?" she asked.

"Home. New York City," I replied.

Where had I visited, she wanted to know. What were the names of people I met? What exactly was my profession? I responded as calmly as I could. She asked me to open the trunk and remain inside my car while she searched it. I complied.

I watched with slowly growing frustration and finally anger as other cars, unsearched, other drivers unquestioned, passed me by. Nervous, beginning to wonder about my own innocence, I suddenly felt the need to justify my activities, my very existence. I remembered having the same feelings when, three years earlier, I was arrested, beaten, and jailed in Tehran [Iran] for the innocent act of walking in a park with a female friend not related to me by blood or marriage.

Returning to her booth, the woman filled out a form, placed my documents in a bag, secured them under my windshield wiper, and instructed me to proceed to the garage behind her booth and remain in the car. My hands over the steering wheel and so out in the open, I waited there, frightened.

Border Search

Minutes later, two armed officers slowly approached my car. Noting their hands over their guns, I flashed on the fear, anxiety, and vulnerability I experienced during my last visit to Iran—my place of birth, my original home. Now, thousands of miles away, the same feelings engulfed me.

"Step out, please," said the officer on the driver's side.

I was asked to open the trunk, take out my bag, and stand beside my car. The officers now just behind me, one to my left, the other to my right, their hands still poised over those guns, escorted me into a building. My every move was closely watched. They were clearly prepared to shoot and I had no doubt I was at the very edge of being under arrest.

I was asked to place my bag on a long metal table, proceed to the counter, remove everything from my pockets and, again, wait. They gave me a form to fill out. Having left my reading glasses in my knapsack, I requested permission to return to the car. On this, they conceded. Cautiously and from a slight distance, they watched me remove my knapsack from the car. Riddled with fear and anger, I stood once again before the counter and filled out the form while one officer emptied my knapsack and the other returned from a search of the car.

Interrogation

Now—the car being clean—they turned to the part of my life that was far harder to search. They questioned me about my identity, activities, exchanges and purchases, friends, travels, and above all whatever made me different from the men and women allowed to zip across the border without a question or a thought. Every card, every piece of paper in my wallet was checked. I was asked to explain my credit card receipts. A bill for five hundred dollars from a small-town garage for the purchase of four new tires aroused suspicion and led to more questioning. A receipt for an airline ticket to Atlanta raised further alarm.

"What was the purpose of your trip to Atlanta?" asked the interrogating officer.

"A book I had written was featured at a conference," I replied. What, he asked suspiciously, might the subject of that book have been?

"Do you travel a lot?" he asked while leafing through the pages of my passport.

With every question, my nervousness increased. I was by now experiencing a regular series of Iran flashbacks. I saw myself back in the custody of the "guardians" of the Islamic Republic. I remembered leaving Iran in July 1999 without even saying farewell to my loved ones. Here at the U.S. border, I fit one uncomfortable "profile"—potential terrorist, Muslim fundamentalist, agent of the Islamic Republic and its global network—there another. I was an activist and critic of the Islamic Republic, a citizen of the United States, and a frequent traveler. In Iran, I fit the profile of agent of the "Great Satan."

The Burden of Homelessness

Thousands of miles away, at the very border of my new home, a haven from the everyday violence of the Islamic Republic, I once again felt like a target. The interrogation was halted mo-

mentarily and I was seated in a corner to await the arrival of a
new officer and yet more questions before I was finally cleared
to proceed.

"Have a good day," said the first officer, and I drove away
from the border.

I had made it back, but for the first time in my life, I
sensed the burden of homelessness that would be the essence
of the next two years of my life as I plunged into a world of
Muslim migrants for whom the search for a home—and profiling of every sort—would be a way of life. Not long after, I
was on the road, looking for and collecting stories from those
who had left their places of birth because of war, violence,
and poverty, but found themselves—unlike me—endlessly
outside the gates of the new homes of which they dreamed.
No one would accept them, nor did most of them have the
option of returning to their places of birth. Many were political refugees; going home would only put their lives in further
danger. Others had spent their life savings on the journey out.
Embarrassed to return empty handed, they felt they had no
choice but to keep going.

Muslim Migrants Searching for a Home

With my own modest border experience in mind, I wondered:
How would they be treated by the border guards and immigration officers who controlled the parapets of the frontiers of
wealth in our world. Just how much would police and citizens, now ever more nervous behind those parapets, view
them as a threat? Just how much of a danger would they
seem, coming as they did from such an unknown and seemingly threatening universe? Months later, the words of a teenage Afghan boy stuck in a makeshift camp in the Greek port
city of Patras—and I heard their equivalent all around the pe-
riphery of Europe—offered me an answer.

> "We are treated like footballs. They kick us, hit us. Why
> don't they just take us to the border and send us back?
> Death is better than this."

That sixteen year-old was typical. He was living in a jerry-rigged tent of plastic and cardboard in a shantytown made up mostly of Afghan refugees and potential immigrants, waiting for his perilous chance to hide in a truck or sneak aboard a ship leaving Greece for Italy. Like many other migrants, his dream was to find a new home in England—a land that, for all he really knew, might as well have been Oz.

For the most part, these migrants had arrived in Greece illegally. Many had applied for asylum, but seeing no chance of being accepted, they were intent on using Greece as a jumping-off spot for launching themselves deeper into Europe, always hoping for a new chance elsewhere. The Greeks, on the other hand, were intent on not letting that happen. Being on the southern end of the European Union (EU), they were tasked with the job of halting the movement of migrants ever deeper into the EU. Greece was then the European Union's gatekeeper and the migrants were to be stopped at all cost. Leaving Greece had to be done clandestinely, away from the watchful eyes of the Greek coastguard officers who were in charge of protecting the harbor—the border—from the stowaways and the illegal travelers. Violators were guaranteed severe punishment.

Stories of Migrants' Treatment

Showing me his broken arm and smiling wistfully, the Afghan boy said, "I slipped under a truck, but they caught me. They came with their sticks and pulled me out, two of them. They began hitting me hard. I was howling. They were using an electric baton and it went on for five or six minutes. After they broke my arm, my friends took me to the hospital."

An Iranian migrant I befriended in Athens had a similar tale. He too had been caught trying to escape to Italy. The coastguard officers had forced him to lie on his belly on the ground, handcuffing his hands behind his back. Then one of them pulled his hair, punched him in the eye, and kicked him in the back. He nearly lost consciousness.

"They took me to an empty bathroom in the harbor, closed the door, and began a second round of beatings. They beat me for twenty minutes, pounding on my face. My chin started bleeding. They hit me with a metal bar. A tourist entered the bathroom and began taking pictures."

That tourist saved the young Iranian, but he would be hospitalized for eight days, his mouth cut in many places. "I was fed intravenously," he told me.

Elsewhere in the EU, and in countries hoping someday to join it, the situation was similar. Among the migrants I met, the Bulgarians were feared the most. An Afghan I ran into in Sofia, the Bulgarian capital, described his encounter with that country's border guards this way:

"I came here illegally from the Turkish border. At the border, I saw the guards set two dogs on someone. He passed out from fear. They really behave in a barbaric way. They beat you ruthlessly. I was caught and deported to Turkey three times. The Turkish guards are better. They take all your money, but they don't beat you like the Bulgarians. As some of my Iraqi friends said, if a war breaks out between Turkey and Bulgaria, they will be the first ones to volunteer to defend Turkey."

But even those who manage to make it past the Greek coastguard or Bulgarian border guards hardly find themselves in the promised land of their dreams. In France, for instance, I found Muslim migrants living in the woods near a highway, like so many hobos during the American Great Depression. A Kurd from Northern Iraq pointed to his shack, a mass of plastic and cardboard held up by sticks, and said, "This is my home. Take a picture of this. We live like animals here." As I photographed his shack, he moved away in shame, adding, "I once had a life."

Muslims Unwelcome Around the World

As I traveled around Europe, I heard ever more testimonies of mistreatment, and met men and women overwhelmed with humiliation and anger—and with no local friends ready to call and offer them aid or protection. These immigrants, at the end of desperate odysseys, remain the unknown victims of September 11—men and women who are suspect simply because of their religion or the place where they were born. On the run from the horrors of war or poverty, looking for a life with just a shred of security, they discover that wherever they arrive, they are completely unwelcome, automatically assumed to be a threat. Beaten or abused, they are interrogated and questioned before being deported as potential terrorists.

I returned to the United States in September 2004, swept away by the stories I had collected. One day not long after, on my way to visit friends in Connecticut, I arrived at New York's Grand Central Station to catch my train. Times had changed. Amid the crowds of travelers were men and women from the National Guard.

Passing the time like so many others until my train was announced, I pulled out my cell phone to call a friend. Still searching the phone for his number, I heard a voice address me. "Can I help you, sir?" Looking up, I saw a woman in uniform. "No, thanks," I replied, surprised. Staring at me for a few seconds, the woman walked away. I looked around, instantly paranoid, feeling all eyes on me. Without thinking, I sat down on some steps, my phone carefully tucked away in my pocket.

Later that day, I told a friend about the encounter. "Oh, the Madrid bombing," he said. The bombs in that city's railway station had been triggered by cell phones, my friend told me. My innocent phone call was a cause for suspicion. I remembered the stories of the many hundred Muslim migrants I had encountered during my journey. This was the world after September 11.

Katrina Exposes American Racism

Clement Alexander Price

Clement Alexander Price is the Board of Governors Distinguished Service Professor of History at Rutgers University. In the following essay, he says that Hurricane Katrina exposed the fault lines of race and class that exist in the United States. He maintains too that, historically, blacks have been more vulnerable than others to natural disasters, and that such phenomena have influenced demographic shifts and the unfolding of contemporary black life.

Like a fire bell in the night, to use Thomas Jefferson's words when he learned of the frightening debate over the Missouri Compromise, many Americans were awakened by the social destruction wrought by Hurricane Katrina when it swept across the Gulf, making landfall on Louisiana, Mississippi, Alabama, and Florida in the late summer of 2005. The storm's aftermath has brought into high relief the enduring fault lines of race, class, and generation. During the first few days of the disaster, electronic and print media provided stark images and testimony of thousands of colored citizens trying to escape cities and towns under water. Indeed, the media actually contributed to the racialized way in which Americans view black people, especially those in trouble and in need of aid. Early on in the crisis, poor blacks were curiously referred to as "refugees" in the media, as if they were from another country. When blacks sought to find food and other essentials after it became clear that assistance was not on the way, they were quickly viewed as looters and common criminals. Through a different lens such behavior by whites was viewed quite differently: they were seeking to survive the aftermath of the storm. As astonished Americans saw the ill fortune shouldered by poor black people in New Orleans, and as far too many of them seemed surprised that modern race relations was implicated in the disaster wrought by Katrina, historians are reminded of an America where natural destruction, social collapse, and sadness have been racialized.

Natural Disasters and Race

Natural disasters in the United States provide a complicated context in which race and racism can be discussed anew. Indeed, although Hurricane Katrina is being exceptionalized as the nation's worst, the social aftermath of the storm is hardly without precedent. The wrath of the natural world, and the seemingly complicit role of powerful leaders on the national and local level, is a part of the nation's history and memory.

More than a century ago, in 1900, the infamous flood in Galveston, Texas, left thousands of residents and settlers vulnerable to water, disease, and the absence of a plan to save lives. The death toll may have been as high as 8,000. Many of the vulnerable ones were blacks at the mercy of a social hierarchy that placed them at or near the bottom. The plight of those who survived has been all but obscured by the timing of their ill fate. The public sphere, as we know it, had not been fully formed. Blacks, Mexicans, poor folks generally, were not given the kind of attention we have become accustomed to. They were all but invisible.

The years that followed the Galveston flood and the other disasters of the early twentieth century—including boll weevil infestation and flooding in the Gulf States—set the stage for the greatest demographic shift of blacks since the last decades of the Trans-Atlantic slave trade, the so-called Great Migration. For years Americans have seen that shift through a rather exceptional lens: Southern blacks, the progeny of slaves, moved out of the South in an attempt to move up. It has been at the center of the modern black narrative, involving countless families, including my own, and the logical place to begin any discussion of black American life. The rise of concentrated black communities in the North, Mid-West and Far West, we have long believed, was the part of the push-and-pull dynamic that simultaneously encouraged blacks to leave the homesteads of their forebears and try life anew, as many migrants said, in "northern country."

The Vulnerability of Blacks and the Poor

Fast forwarding to Katrina, we might want to reconsider how the pervasiveness of natural disasters influenced the way modern and contemporary black life unfolded. Perhaps the unpredictability of nature's wrath should be factored into our perception of the American past, when blacks seem to be disproportionately vulnerable, when they are buffeted by the winds, the waters, and public indifference. Recent scholarship does indeed suggest that poor people are disproportionately at greater risk during disastrous episodes like hurricanes and floods, are less prepared when disaster strikes, and face greater destruction to home and hearth when compared to those with more substantial means.

The last century's most devastating natural disasters were preludes to what we grimly witnessed when Katrina hit and when its aftermath intersected with race, class, and human indifference to the proper stewardship of land and water. That natural disaster brought into high relief the ebb and flow of American race relations and the vulnerability of black Americans when their private lives rely on public response. Many have left their destroyed homes and communities, probably never to return as residents.

It is a sad reality that the public sphere, which African Americans have long sought to ennoble and empower as the common ground for equality and justice, continues to be racialized against the individual and collective interests of black and brown citizens of the Republic. Such is Katrina's legacy, and the legacy of race when storms and other destructive natural forces hit areas where black communities exist all too poorly.

CHAPTER 3

Race and
U.S. Institutions

In Defense of Racial Profiling

Michelle Malkin

Michelle Malkin, a conservative political and social commentator, is the author of In Defense of Internment: The Case for "Racial Profiling" in World War II and the War on Terror. *In the following essay, she argues that, post-9/11, racial profiling of Arab Americans is justified and even necessary for American security.*

When our national security is on the line, "racial profiling"—or more precisely, threat profiling based on race, religion or nationality—is justified. Targeted intelligence-gathering at mosques and in local Muslim communities, for example, makes perfect sense when we are at war with Islamic extremists.

Yet, [in August 2004] the FBI came under fire for questioning Muslims in Seattle about possible terrorist ties. Members of a local mosque complained to Rep. Jim McDermott, D-Wash., who called for a congressional investigation of the FBI's innocuous tactics. The American Civil Liberties Union of Washington accused the agency of "ethnic profiling."

But where else are federal agents supposed to turn for help in uncovering terrorist plots by Islamic fanatics: Buddhist temples? Knights of Columbus meetings? Amish neighborhoods?

Some might argue that profiling is so offensive to fundamental American values that it ought to be prohibited, even if the prohibition jeopardizes our safety. Yet many of the ethnic activists and civil-liberties groups who object most strenuously to the use of racial, ethnic, religious and nationality

Michelle Malkin, "Racial Profiling: A Matter of Survival," *USA Today*, August 16, 2004. Copyright 2004 USA Today, a division of Gannett Co., Inc. Reproduced by permission of Michelle Malkin for text entries and Creators Syndicate, Inc.

classifications during war support the use of similar classifications to ensure "diversity" or "parity" in peacetime.

The civil-rights hypocrites have never met a "compelling government interest" for using racial, ethnicity or nationality classifications they didn't like, except when that compelling interest happens to be the nation's very survival.

Missed Opportunities

Consider what happened in summer 2001, when Phoenix FBI agent Kenneth Williams urged his superiors to investigate militant Muslim men whom he suspected of training in U.S. flight schools as part of al-Qaeda missions.

Williams' recommendation was rejected, FBI Director Robert Mueller later said, partly because of concerns that the plan could be viewed as discriminatory racial profiling.

Mueller acknowledged that if Williams' Phoenix profiling memo had been shared with the agency's Minneapolis office, which had unsuccessfully sought a special intelligence warrant to search suspected terrorist Zacarias Moussaoui's laptop computer, the warrant might have been granted.

If the FBI had taken Williams' advice, the feeling of some Arabs and Muslims might have been hurt. But the Twin Towers might still be standing and 3,000 innocent people might be alive today.

Absolutists who oppose national-security profiling often invoke the World War II experience of Japanese-Americans. When asked whether the 12 Muslim chaplains serving in the armed forces should be vetted more carefully than military rabbis or priests, Sarah Eltantawi of the Muslim Public Affairs Council raised the specter of Japanese internment.

The analogy is ridiculous. The more extensive screening of 12 military officers is a far cry from the evacuation of 112,000 individuals on the West Coast. The targeted profiling of Muslims serving in sensitive positions is not a constitutional crisis.

Some argue that the dismissal of charges against Army Capt. James Yee, a former Muslim chaplain who ministered to enemy combatants at Guantanamo Bay, Cuba, and was initially suspected of espionage, undermines the case for profiling of any kind. Not at all. As the Defense Department has acknowledged, the military's 12 Muslim chaplains were trained by a radical Wahhabi school and were certified by a Muslim group founded by Abdurahman Alamoudi, who was charged in September 2003 with accepting hundreds of thousands of dollars from Libya, a U.S.-designated sponsor of terrorism. These associations cannot be ignored.

Unfortunately, the Pentagon caved in to Eltantawi and her fellow travelers. Rather than focus exclusively on the 12 Muslim chaplains, it pressed forward with a review of all 2,800 military chaplains.

The refusal to be discriminating was, as Sen. Jon Kyl, R-Ariz., acknowledged, the "height of politically correct stupidity."

Smoke-and-Mirrors Arguments

In the wake of 9/11, opponents of profiling have shifted away from arguing against it because it is "racist" and now claim that it endangers security because it is a drain on resources and damages relations with ethnic and religious minorities, thereby hampering intelligence-gathering. These assertions are cleverly fine-tuned to appeal to post-9/11 sensibilities, but they are unfounded and disingenuous. The fact that al-Qaeda is using some non-Arab recruits does not render profiling moot. As long as we have open borders, Osama bin Laden will continue to send Middle East terrorists here by land, sea and air. Profiling is just one discretionary investigative tool among many.

Post-9/11, the belief that racial, religious and nationality profiling is never justified has become a dangerous bugaboo. It is unfortunate that loyal Muslims or Arabs might be burdened because of terrorists who share their race, nationality or religion. But any inconvenience is preferable to suffering a second mass terrorist attack on American soil.

Racial Profiling
Is Never Justified

Cathy Young

Cathy Young is a columnist for the Boston Globe. *In the following essay, she argues against the right-wing commentator Michelle Malkin, who maintains that racial profiling is necessary in order to protect the United States against potential terrorists. Young says that the profiling used in World War II to intern Japanese Americans was a national embarrassment, and that rehabilitating the racial policies that were used during that time of national crisis would be a grave mistake. Young sees Malkin's position as a response to leftist commentators who have been highly critical of the United States, and she laments the lack of decency surrounding the debate between conservatives and liberals on questions of race and ideology.*

During World War II, the U.S. government interned about 120,000 ethnic Japanese living in America, two-thirds of whom were U.S. citizens. This is almost universally regarded as a shameful blot on America's history, a cautionary tale of racism, paranoia, and wartime hysteria. In 1988 President [Ronald] Reagan called it "a grave wrong" and signed legislation authorizing $20,000 in reparations to each surviving internee.

In 2000 another eminent conservative, Supreme Court Justice Antonin Scalia, assailed his colleagues' ruling striking down Nebraska's late-term abortion ban by likening it to *Dred Scott* and *Korematsu*, the rulings which upheld the constitutionality of, respectively, slavery and the Japanese-American internment.

Defending a Reviled Policy

So it takes some nerve to pen a defense of this reviled policy—which is exactly what the author and syndicated columnist Michelle Malkin did recently, in a new book titled *In Defense of Internment: The Case for "Racial Profiling" in World War II and the War on Terror*. Malkin's argument is closely tied to post–September 11 debates about ethnic, racial, and religious profiling as a "homeland security" measure.

Inevitably, critics have raised the Japanese internment as an extreme case of racial profiling gone awry. Malkin believes our safety is being compromised because any common-sense proposal that involves profiling—be it extra-vigilant screening of Middle Eastern passengers at airports, targeted monitoring of visitors with guest visas from countries with terrorist links, or special scrutiny of Muslim chaplains in the armed forces—is shouted down by invoking the specter of internment camps. And it's true that internment parallels have been frivolously and promiscuously thrown about in this debate.

One would think, though, that if you truly wanted to counter such slippery-slope hyperbole about ethnic or religious profiling, the last thing you'd want to do would be to defend internment. It's a bit like trying to counter arguments that legalized abortion leads to acceptance of infanticide by publishing a tract in defense of infanticide. Malkin's calculus, however, is different: She hopes that if Americans can be persuaded to get over the Japanese internment guilt complex, the profiling of Arab Americans and Muslims will become more acceptable.

Debunking "Politically Correct Myths"

To counter this guilt complex—peddled, according to Malkin, by high school textbooks, universities, ethnic activists, politicians, and the media—Malkin sets out to debunk what she describes as politically correct myths about internment: that it was motivated primarily by racism and hysteria, that there was no national security justification for it, and that the relocation and internment camps were Nazi-style death camps. (It's not clear who has ever made that last claim. Malkin asserts simply that such images are evoked today by the use of the term *concentration camp*, a phrase that was actually used by U.S. authorities at the time.)

The truth, Malkin contends, is that the U.S. leadership had ample reason to fear sabotage and espionage by ethnic Japanese—particularly on the basis of intelligence data declassified years after the war, from decoded Japanese diplomatic communications—and didn't have the ability or the resources to assess individual risk.

Historical Revisionism

As historical revisionism, *In Defense of Internment* largely falls flat. (You can go to isthatlegal.org for two scholars' critique of the book, and to Malkin's own site, michellemalkin.com, for her replies. . . .) Malkin does demonstrate that there were instances of disloyalty by Japanese aliens and Japanese Americans during the war, and that the [Franklin] Roosevelt administration had evidence that the Japanese military was seeking, apparently with some success, to recruit agents in the Japanese community on the West Coast of the United States. But she never justifies a response as extreme, and as offensive to the most basic notions of justice and human rights, as mass internment.

Anti-Japanese Bigotry

Of the anti-Japanese bigotry that was pervasive in America and especially on the West Coast even *before* Pearl Harbor, and was whipped up into virulent hate by a propaganda campaign after the start of the war, Malkin says nary a word.

Responding to critics on her blog, she suggests she didn't need to address the issue of racism because her whole point was to disprove the "myth" that it was a dominant factor in the internment. (In other words, if you decide to write a book debunking the notion that obesity causes heart disease, you can omit any mention of obesity in your examination of risk factors. Makes sense.)

In the same vein, Malkin gives only passing mention to such unpleasantness as shootings of internees by camp guards but discusses at length the amenities offered in the camps and the petty complaints of some internees.

Debunking "The Myth of McCarthyism"

In a way, *In Defense of Internment* follows in the footsteps of another recent famous (or infamous) right-wing tome: [2003's] *Treason*, by Ann Coulter, which undertook the rehabilitation of Sen. Joseph McCarthy and a debunking of "the myth of 'McCarthyism.'" McCarthy, Coulter proclaimed, was a true hero in the struggle against communism, and the only unjust persecution was that of Tail Gunner Joe himself by his left-wing, America-hating enemies.

There's a strong parallel between Coulter's apologia for the anti-communist witch hunts and Malkin's apologia for the Japanese-American internment: In both cases, there was a genuine national security risk *and* a wrongheaded, hysterical government response that did grave damage to the very freedoms it was supposed to protect.

Notably, Coulter's harshest critics include anti-communist historians, such as Ronald Radosh and Harvey Klehr, who have taken a lot of flak from their left-wing colleagues for daring to say that Soviet espionage really was a serious threat and that many American Communists targeted as Soviet agents really were guilty. Radosh referred to *Treason* as "crap" on Andrew Sullivan's weblog, expressing dismay that Coulter drew on his work to support her "ludicrous" arguments. Klehr, writing in *The New Republic*, dismissed her book as a "crass apologia for McCarthyism."

Skewering Sacred Cows

Why the rush to defend what was only recently seen, across the political spectrum, as indefensible? Partly, it's the sheer appeal and satisfaction of skewering sacred cows, liberal ones especially—and there are, God knows, so many that deserve skewering. Indeed, in the case of McCarthyism, the stubborn blindness of leftists and many liberals both to the brutality of the Soviet regime and to the extent of Soviet espionage during the Cold War undoubtedly helped create fertile ground for Coulter-style polemics.

A similar dynamic may be at work with the Japanese internment issue. Some of the history textbooks Malkin indignantly quotes probably do err on the side of dismissing all World War II–era concerns about subversive activities by Japanese ethnics as unfounded paranoia. The weakness of this position creates an opening for revisionism, including the radical revisionism of *In Defense of Internment*.

Liberals, Conservatives, and Decency

It is useful, too, to remember that defending the indefensible has long been a popular sport on the left, whose own revisionist historians are busy trying to sugarcoat not McCarthyism but Stalinism.

Also at work, however, is the dark side of modern American conservatism. The left's obsession with America's allegedly unique evilness, and in particular with real or imagined racism, has prompted a fully justified backlash. But that backlash can morph into an ugly and disturbing mind-set—one that regards all efforts to confront America's past wrongs as the province of sissy liberals and wild-eyed lefties.

As the revisionists plow ahead, sometimes one wants to ask, "Have you no sense of decency, folks, at long last? Have you left no sense of decency?"

The Legacy of Disadvantage in the United States

Alan Greenblatt

Alan Greenblatt is a staff writer at Governing *magazine. In the following essay he asks to what extent racism is still a problem for U.S. blacks even after schools have been integrated and race-based discrimination outlawed. He says that, unfortunately, even in the twenty-first century, the legacy of racism affects blacks' economic and educational opportunities, as well as their access to housing and medical care. He surveys data to show how different races in the United States fare and how American institutions, which are predominantly white, set the standard for how its citizens perform and succeed.*

When Joe Moore got out of jail in June, the 60-year-old hog farmer told reporters, "I just want to go home, look at TV and stay out of trouble." After her release, Kizzie White, 26, hugged her two children and said, "I'm going to be the best mother I can to them."

Moore and White were among the more than three-dozen, mostly black residents of the West Texas town of Tulia convicted of drug crimes four years ago solely on the now-discredited testimony of an undercover police officer widely labeled as a racist.

Race Still Matters

Many white Americans believe that race no longer matters in America, now that public schools have been integrated, blacks can vote and race-based job and housing discrimination are illegal. Yet racial incidents like Tulia continue to erupt, periodically shattering Americans' complacency about race and signaling to many observers that racist sentiments still linger in some psyches.

Often the eruptions spill into the streets—usually in response to allegedly racist police actions—such as the riots that broke out in Cincinnati in April 2001 or in Benton Harbor, Mich., this past June [2003].

Lately, some of the incidents—particularly in the South—appear to represent a longing by some for the pre-1960s era of segregation. In Georgia this spring, white high-school students held a prom at which African-American students pointedly were excluded—a year after the school's first integrated prom. That followed the downfall last fall of Sen. Trent Lott of Mississippi, who was forced to resign as majority leader after saying America would have been better off if then-Gov. Strom Thurmond of South Carolina had won the presidency in 1948, when he was an ardent segregationist.

And some of the racially tinged incidents have been particularly conscience-searing: the murder of James Byrd Jr., chained behind a truck in Jasper, Texas, and dragged to death; the broomstick sodomizing of Haitian immigrant Abner Louima and the shooting of unarmed African immigrant Amadou Diallo by New York policemen; the beating in Los Angeles of Rodney King.

Differing Views on Race

Such cases bring into dramatic focus the often diametrically opposing ways in which whites and blacks view race relations in America, especially when the criminal-justice system is involved. Many whites saw the acquittal of O.J. Simpson in the murder of his ex-wife Nicole Simpson and her friend Ron Goldman as a miscarriage of justice, while blacks generally viewed it as a triumph over racist police tactics. Similarly, blacks in Tulia celebrated the release of their fellow citizens as righting a racial injustice while whites continued to question the prisoners' innocence.

And even the Supreme Court's landmark approval recently of the University of Michigan's use of affirmative action in law-school admissions was viewed differently by some blacks and whites.

Blacks Are Still Trailing Whites

But many Americans—whites as well as blacks—say the nation's racial problems go beyond racial preferences and the criminal-justice system. They say discrimination still exists despite civil-rights laws, undercutting blacks educationally and economically. Although African-Americans have made economic, political and social progress over the last four decades, by several objective measures they are trailing whites:

- Median income among black men is only 73 percent as high as that of white men, and only 84 percent for black women compared with white women.

- Blacks are 60 percent less likely than whites to receive access to sophisticated medical treatments such as coronary angioplasty and bypass surgery.

- Minorities are far more likely to pay higher, "predatory" mortgage rates than whites.

- A majority of black students score below the basic level in five out of seven subject areas on the National Assessment of Educational Progress (NAEP) tests, compared to only about 20 percent of white students.

- One in five black men spends part of his life in prison—seven times the rate for whites. Blacks are 13 percent of the U.S. population, but make up more than 40 percent of the prisoners on Death Row. . . .

Racial Divide in Education

Gary Orfield, co-director of the Harvard Civil Rights Project, says the racial divide still appears to be widest in public education. Despite decades of court-ordered school integration, more than one in six black children attends a school comprised of 99–100 percent minority students; by comparison, less than 1 percent of white public-school students attend such schools.

Many observers have expected the Republican Party to adopt a more conciliatory stance toward blacks, who overwhelmingly favor Democrats in elections for all levels of office. Indeed, a day after 12 of the Tulia defendants were released from prison, the Bush administration barred federal officers from using race or ethnicity as a factor in conducting investigations (except in cases involving terrorism or national security).

But some African-American leaders question the Bush administration's commitment to fighting racism. "Bush represents anathema to our struggle for social justice," says civil-rights activist Jesse Jackson. "He would not permit [secretary of state Colin] Powell to go to the U.N. conference on racism in South Africa; he has sought to stock the courts with anti-civil rights judges; he is anti-affirmative action. . . . We are simply on different teams."

Less than a month after Lott stepped down, President [George W.] Bush spoke out against the University of Michigan's use of racial preferences.

Bush's supporters, however, say he has appointed as many women and minorities to top government jobs as Bill Clinton, whose administration was the most racially diverse in history. "The president is very committed to diversity of thought, of professional background, of geography, ethnicity and gender," said Clay Johnson, who coordinated appointments for Bush. By March 2001, he noted, 27 percent of Bush's selections were women, and 20 to 25 percent were minorities.

"Race-Neutral Policies" and "Black Advantage?"

Like many conservatives, Bush believes that the interests of blacks, as well as whites, are best served by race-neutral policies. "As we work to address the wrong of racial prejudice, we must not use means that create another wrong, and thus perpetuate our divisions," he said.

Indeed, Heather Mac Donald, a senior fellow at the Manhattan Institute, says "the white establishment is doing everything it can to hire as many black employees as it can. If you are a black high-school student who graduates with modest SATs today, you're going to have colleges beating down your door to try and persuade you to come."

But David Wellman, a white professor of community studies at the University of California, Santa Cruz, sees an opposite reality. "Race not only matters, but whites have an advantage because blacks have a disadvantage," says Wellman, coauthor of the forthcoming book *Whitewashing Race.* "That's the dirty little secret that nobody wants to talk about anymore.

"Everyone wants to believe that racism has been essentially solved through legislation," he insists. "Unfortunately, when you look at the evidence in terms of education, crime and welfare, it's just shocking how important race continues to be."

Blacks to Blame for Their Disadvantage?

Some scholars argue that, absent overt discrimination, blacks must share much of the blame if their circumstances are not equal to whites. "The grip of the Cult of Victimology encourages the black American from birth to fixate upon remnants of racism and resolutely downplay all signs of its demise," writes John McWhorter, a professor at the University of California, Berkeley.

Faith Mitchell, deputy director of the National Research Council's Division on Behavioral and Social Sciences, acknowledges that her fellow African-Americans have made much progress—but only to a point. "Yes, you have a growing black middle class," she says, "but it's still disproportionately small relative to the rest of the black population. The lower class is growing faster." . . .

Is Discrimination Still a Problem in the United States?

In 1988, when a residential treatment center opened in Indianapolis for convicted child molesters, neighbors accepted it with little comment. But three years later, when it was converted into a facility for homeless veterans—half of them black—neighborhood whites vandalized a car and burned a cross.

"An all-white cadre of child molesters was evidently acceptable," wrote Randall Kennedy, a black Harvard law-school professor, "but the presence of blacks made a racially integrated group of homeless veterans intolerable!"

The Indianapolis case was unusually overt, says Leonard Steinhorn, an American University professor and coauthor of the book *By the Color of Our Skin: The Illusion of Integration and the Reality of Race*. Most opposition to racial integration is much more subtle, he says. "Today, a black person moves in and most white people accept it, or even like it," Steinhorn says. "But one or two families get nervous and move out. More blacks may move in, because they see that the first blacks have been accepted. Then a couple more whites say we better move.

"It's a slow and gradual phenomenon, not the spontaneous, overnight reaction we saw in the past," Steinhorn explains. Even if the African-Americans share the same socioeconomic footing as the whites, most whites will not stay in a neighborhood once it becomes more than 10 to 15 percent black, he says.

But some observers argue that segregation today is more a matter of choice than of bigotry. "White flight is just as widespread as ever," says Jared Taylor, editor of *American Renais-*

sance magazine, who has been described as a white nationalist. "Even if few people acknowledge it, people prefer the company of people like themselves, and race is an important ingredient. Given the chance, they spend their time in homogeneous groups. It is part of human nature."

Taylor's sentiments are echoed by Carol Swain, a black professor of law and political science at Vanderbilt University. "Clearly, discrimination exists, and in very subtle ways," she says, but it is "human nature for people to favor their own group." Indeed, many "black separatists" argue that African-Americans can achieve more by running their own businesses in their own communities, rather than seeking opportunities among whites.

"I would prefer to see more integration," says Bob Zelnick, chairman of the Boston University journalism department and a member of the conservative Citizens' Initiative on Race and Ethnicity. "But I don't think it's a mark of failure if people prefer to live among their own kind. There's some lingering discrimination [in the United States], but I think the determined middle-class or upper-middle-class minority family that seeks to live in a white neighborhood can do so." . . .

Meanwhile, Harvard history Professor Stephan Thernstrom says studies show residential segregation has been declining since the 1960s. "[Segregation] is now at the lowest level since 1920," he says. Real estate agents and home sellers are more interested in closing the deal than engaging in discrimination. If residential segregation exists, he says, it's largely a matter of choice.

But some racial separation may not be by mutual choice. A recent Urban Institute analysis of home-loan applications in Chicago and Los Angeles found that information was withheld from blacks and Hispanics in "statistically significant patterns of unequal treatment" that "systematically favor whites." In another study, African-American women had access to about half as many rental properties as white males because of disparities in the information the women received. . . .

Moreover, American University's Steinhorn says, many forms of de facto discrimination still are practiced today, such as requiring black job applicants—but not whites—to take writing tests; department store security guards following blacks more closely than whites; and drug stores failing to carry African-American hair-care products to discourage their patronage.

"It doesn't have to be legalized, high-profile segregation to be meaningful," Steinhorn says. "This is the stuff of life. If it's death by a thousand cuts, that's as powerful as being told you have to sit at the back of the bus."

Are Blacks Still Economically Disadvantaged Due to Racism?

Nearly everyone agrees that blacks, generally, are far better off financially than they were 40 years ago. But blacks still hold a fraction of whites' accumulated assets. For instance, the proportion of blacks that own their own homes has doubled since 1940, but it is still about a third below the rate for whites.

Are these financial disparities between the races due to racism or to socioeconomic factors and differences in education levels? Steinhorn and others say the persistent separation of the races has negative financial consequences for blacks. Segregation, for instance, can prevent blacks from having access to the social networks that can lead to good jobs. Some economists also argue that urban blacks suffer from "spatial mismatch"—unequal access to suburban jobs located near white residential areas. High crime rates also hamper black wealth creation.

"Crime depresses the property values in cities and neighborhoods that blacks tend to live in," says George R. La Noue, a political scientist at the University of Maryland, Baltimore County.

Much of the racial disparity in wealth is the result of the historical legacy of segregation, according to Steinhorn and others. Black families simply have not had time to accrue wealth to match the generations of inherited property and other assets enjoyed by whites. Blacks also have a harder time investing in major assets, such as real estate.

"There is no question that minorities are less likely than whites to obtain mortgage financing and that, if successful, they receive less generous loan amounts and terms," concluded a 1999 Urban Institute study.

Education is perhaps the biggest factor affecting black incomes. Blacks consistently trail behind whites on standardized tests, and people who achieve higher test scores usually can command higher salaries.

But the University of California's McWhorter says the disparity in education levels can't be attributed solely to racism. "A cultural trait is the driving factor in depressing black scholarly performance," he writes. "A wariness of books and learning for learning's sake as [being] 'white' has become ingrained in black American culture."

Harvard's Thernstrom, co-author of a forthcoming book on racial disparities in education, *No Excuses: Closing the Racial Gap in Learning,* says the education gap largely explains the income gap. Too many studies unfairly compare income levels for blacks and whites who have completed the same level of education, he argues. But blacks score more poorly on standardized tests than whites at the same grade level, indicating that they are not receiving the same level of instruction.

"When you measure educational achievement—not by the time you've spent under a school roof, but by what you know—the disparity in racial income mostly disappears," he says. "People of different races with equal levels of cognitive skills have earned about the same amount of money in our society for the past 25 years. Even if employers aren't discriminating at all on the basis of race, they are paying higher-skilled workers more."

Thernstrom believes that blacks' poor test scores are not so much due to racism but to flaws in K–12 public education in general. He says concentrating efforts on improving schools would aid education in general while also aiding blacks and other minorities.

"In a society committed to equal opportunity, we still have a racially identifiable group of educational have-nots—young African-Americans and Latinos," write Thernstrom and his wife and co-author, Abigail Thernstrom, a senior fellow at the Manhattan Institute and a member of the U.S. Civil Rights Commission. "They place some blame on members of these groups for failing to place an emphasis on education and for a cultural work ethic that sometimes equates achievement with acting white or selling out."

But the Thernstroms place heavier blame on schools for failing to adapt to group cultural differences and for not demanding high standards from their students. "Plenty of white and Asian kids are also being shortchanged," they write, "but it is the black and Hispanic [statistics] that suggest appalling indifference."

Many people on the other side, however, citing the recent New York appeals court decision, point out that American school-funding policies—which unlike any other industrialized country are based on property values—are clearly lopsided against poorer school districts, which often are made up primarily of blacks, Latinos and other minorities.

However, William E. Spriggs, executive director of the National Urban League's Institute for Opportunity and Equality, says even highly educated blacks suffer higher unemployment rates than whites. "Year after year, the unemployment rate for [black] college graduates has continued to climb," Spriggs says, "whereas for whites, it's been fairly stable." . . .

Is the Criminal Justice System Racially Biased?

Black comedian Richard Pryor used to joke about going to court seeking justice in America. "And that's exactly what I saw," he said. "Just us."

Indeed, blacks comprise 13 percent of the country's population but more than 40 percent of the U.S. prison population, according to the Washington-based Sentencing Project. A black male born in 1991 stands a 29 percent chance of spending time in prison, compared with 4 percent for white males. In 1995, one in three black men between the ages of 20 and 29 was either in prison, on probation or on parole.

Many African-Americans argue that more blacks are in jail because police and prosecutors target blacks. Many blacks say they have been pulled over for the "crime" of "driving while black." "Nothing has poisoned race relations more," writes Harvard's Kennedy, "than racially discriminatory policing, pursuant to which blacks are watched, questioned and detained more than others."

Lawsuits challenging the constitutionality of racial profiling have led to settlements in California, Maryland and other states, many of which have revised their policies for stopping motorists. In March, New Jersey became the first state to ban profiling. And in June [2003] President Bush banned racial profiling at the federal level—except in cases involving terrorism and national security. . . .

In a widely cited study, Michael Tonry, director of the University of Cambridge's Institute of Criminology, maintains that more blacks are locked up because they commit more "imprisonable crimes."

Perhaps more poignantly, Jesse Jackson once said, "There is nothing more painful for me at this stage in my life than to walk down the street and hear footsteps and start to think about robbery and see it's somebody white and feel relieved."

Still, some critics say when blacks do commit crimes, they can't get a fair shake from the criminal-justice system. Although even critics of the system admit that data is scarce comparing how blacks and whites are sentenced for committing the same crimes, the University of California's Wellman cites studies in Georgia and New York that show racial differences in the prison terms imposed for similar offenses.

Members of the Congressional Black Caucus—including Rep. John Conyers, D-Mich., the ranking Democrat on the Judiciary Committee—often complain that sentencing guidelines are much harsher for crack cocaine, predominantly used and sold by blacks, than for powder cocaine, used primarily by whites. But critics of that argument note the Black Caucus pushed hard for tough laws against crack precisely because it is a scourge in predominantly black communities.

But the biggest disparities result because of where police concentrate their enforcement efforts, says Mark Mauer, assistant director of the Sentencing Project. "Drug use and abuse cuts across race and class lines, but drug-law enforcement is primarily located in the inner cities," Mauer says. Moreover, he points out, white suburban teenagers caught with drugs might be sent to treatment programs instead of being prosecuted, but similar treatment isn't offered to blacks: "In a low-income community, those resources aren't provided to the same extent, so [drug possession] is much more likely to be defined as a criminal-justice problem."

Critics of the criminal-justice system also argue that street crimes are prosecuted more harshly than white-collar crimes, which primarily are committed by whites. But that's because tax fraud and securities abuse are less of a societal concern than armed robbery, says Harvard sociologist Christopher Jencks. "Given a choice, almost everyone would rather be robbed by a computer than at gunpoint," he writes.

Racial disparities also exist in the use of the death penalty, according to a recent Maryland study. It found that blacks who murdered whites were far more likely to face the death penalty than either white killers or blacks who killed other blacks. A court-appointed committee in Pennsylvania announced in March that the state should halt executions pending a study of racial bias. Several other states have commissioned studies to determine whether the death penalty is applied more often or unfairly to blacks.

"Generally, discrimination based on the race of the defendant has tremendously declined," says David Baldus, a University of Iowa law professor who has studied racial bias in the death penalty. "But discrimination based on the race of victim has continued."

The Dominance of Asian Americans in Higher Education

Timothy Egan

Timothy Egan is a national enterprise reporter for the New York Times. *In the following essay, he discusses the overwhelming presence of Asian Americans in top-ranked American universities, including the University of California at Berkeley. Ten years after California passed Proposition 209, voting to eliminate racial preferences in the public sector, the number of Asian students has grown, at the expense of already underrepresented blacks and Hispanics. And what is happening at Berkeley is mirrored all over the country: With the elimination of affirmative action and admissions based on merit alone, Asian Americans make up less than 5 percent of the population but typically make up 10 to 30 percent of students at the nation's best colleges. Egan asks why this situation has come about, whether something should be done to stop the trend, and what it implies for the future of American education.*

When Jonathan Hu was going to high school in suburban Southern California, he rarely heard anyone speaking Chinese. But striding through campus on his way to class at the University of California, Berkeley, Mr. Hu hears Mandarin all the time, in plazas, cafeterias, classrooms, study halls, dorms and fast-food outlets. It is part of the soundtrack at this iconic university, along with Cantonese, English, Spanish and, of course, the perpetual jackhammers from the perpetual construction projects spurred by the perpetual fund drives.

"Here, many people speak Chinese as their primary language," says Mr. Hu, a sophomore. "It's nice. You really feel like you don't stand out."

Today, he is iPod-free, a rare condition on campus, taking in the early winter sun at the dour concrete plaza of the Free Speech Movement Cafe, named for the protests led by Mario Savio in 1964, when the administration tried to muzzle political activity. "Free speech marks us off from the stones and stars," reads a Savio quote on the cafe wall, "just below the angels."

There are now mostly small protests, against the new chain stores invading Telegraph Avenue, just outside the campus entrance, and to save the old oak trees scheduled for removal so the football stadium can be renovated. The biggest buzz on Telegraph one week was the grand opening of a chain restaurant—the new Chipotle's, which drew a crowd of students eager to get in. The scent of patchouli oil and reefer is long gone; the street is posted as a drug-free zone.

And at least on this morning, there is very little speech of any kind inside the Free Speech Cafe; almost without exception, students are face-planted in their laptops, silently downloading class notes, music, messages. It could be the library but for the line for lattes. On mornings like this, the public university beneath the towering campanile seems like a small, industrial city of über-students in flops.

Selective Self-Segregation on an Overwhelmingly Asian Campus

I ask Mr. Hu what it's like to be on a campus that is overwhelmingly Asian—what it's like to be of the demographic moment. This fall and last, the number of Asian freshmen at Berkeley has been at a record high, about 46 percent. The overall undergraduate population is 41 percent Asian. On this golden campus, where a creek runs through a redwood grove, there are residence halls with Asian themes; good dim sum is never more than a five-minute walk away; heaping, spicy bowls of pho are served up in the Bear's Lair cafeteria; and numerous social clubs are linked by common ancestry to countries far across the Pacific.

Mr. Hu shrugs, saying there is a fair amount of "selective self-racial segregation," which is not unusual at a university this size: about 24,000 undergraduates. "The different ethnic groups don't really interact that much," he says. "There's definitely a sense of sticking with your community." But, he quickly adds, "People of my generation don't look at race as that big of a deal. People here, the freshmen and sophomores, they're pretty much like your average American teenagers."

Spend a few days at Berkeley, on the classically manicured slope overlooking San Francisco Bay and the distant Pacific, and soon enough the sound of foreign languages becomes less distinct. This is a global campus in a global age. And more than any time in its history, it looks toward the setting sun for its identity.

The revolution at Berkeley is a quiet one, a slow turning of the forces of immigration and demographics. What is troubling to some is that the big public school on the hill certainly does not look like the ethnic face of California, which is 12 percent Asian, more than twice the national average. But it is the new face of the state's vaunted public university system. Asians make up the largest single ethnic group, 37 percent, at its nine undergraduate campuses.

The oft-cited goal of a public university is to be a microcosm—in this case, of the nation's most populous, most demographically dynamic state—and to enrich the educational experience with a variety of cultures, economic backgrounds and viewpoints.

The Rise of the Asian Campus

But 10 years after California passed Proposition 209, voting to eliminate racial preferences in the public sector, university administrators find such balance harder to attain. At the same time, affirmative action is being challenged on a number of new fronts, in court and at state ballot boxes. And elite colleges have recently come under attack for practicing it—specifically, for bypassing highly credentialed Asian applicants in favor of students of color with less stellar test scores and grades.

In California, the rise of the Asian campus, of the strict meritocracy, has come at the expense of historically underrepresented blacks and Hispanics. This year [2007], in a class of 4,809, there are only 100 black freshmen at the University of California at Los Angeles—the lowest number in 33 years. At Berkeley, 3.6 percent of freshmen are black, barely half the statewide proportion. (In 1997, just before the full force of Proposition 209 went into effect, the proportion of black freshmen matched the state population, 7 percent.) The percentage of Hispanic freshmen at Berkeley (11 percent) is not even a third of the state proportion (35 percent). White freshmen (29 percent) are also below the state average (44 percent).

This is in part because getting into Berkeley—*U.S. News & World Report*'s top-ranked public university—has never been more daunting. There were 41,750 applicants for this year's freshman class of 4,157. Nearly half had a weighted grade point average of 4.0 or better (weighted for advanced courses). There is even grumbling from "the old Blues"—older alumni named for the school color—"who complain because their kids can't get in," says Gregg Thomson, director of the Office of Student Research.

Mr. Hu applied to a lot of colleges, but Berkeley felt right for him from the start. "It's the intellectual atmosphere—this place is intense."

Mr. Hu says he was pressured by a professor to go into something like medicine or engineering. "It's a stereotype, but a lot of Asians who come here just study engineering and the sciences," he says. "I was never interested in that."

But as the only son of professionals born in China, Mr. Hu fits the profile of Asians at Berkeley in at least one way: they are predominantly first-generation American. About 95 percent of Asian freshmen come from a family in which one or both parents were born outside the United States.

He dashes off to class, and I wander through the serene setting of Memorial Glade, in the center of campus, and then loop over to Sproul Plaza, the beating heart of the university, where dozens of tables are set up by clubs representing every conceivable ethnic group. Out of nowhere, an a cappella group, mostly Asian men, appears and starts singing a Beach Boys song. Yes, tradition still matters in California.

Across the United States, at elite private and public universities, Asian enrollment is near an all-time high. Asian-Americans make up less than 5 percent of the population but typically make up 10 to 30 percent of students at the nation's best colleges: in 2005, the last year with across-the-board numbers, Asians made up 24 percent of the undergraduate population at Carnegie Mellon and at Stanford, 27 percent at the Massachusetts Institute of Technology, 14 percent at Yale and 13 percent at Princeton.

And according to advocates of race-neutral admissions policies, those numbers should be even higher.

The "New Jews"

Asians have become the "new Jews," in the phrase of Daniel Golden, whose recent book, *The Price of Admission: How America's Ruling Class Buys Its Way into Elite Colleges—and Who Gets Left Outside the Gates,* is a polemic against university admissions policies. Mr. Golden, a reporter for the *Wall Street Journal,* is referring to evidence that, in the first half of the 20th century, Ivy League schools limited the number of Jewish students despite their outstanding academic records to maintain the primacy of upper-class Protestants. Today, he writes, "Asian-Americans are the odd group out, lacking racial preferences enjoyed by other minorities and the advantages of wealth and lineage mostly accrued by upper-class whites. Asians are typecast in college admissions offices as quasi-robots programmed by their parents to ace math and science."

As if to illustrate the point, a study released in October by the Center for Equal Opportunity, an advocacy group opposing race-conscious admissions, showed that in 2005 Asian-Americans were admitted to the University of Michigan, Ann Arbor, at a much lower rate (54 percent) than black applicants (71 percent) and Hispanic applicants (79 percent)—despite median SAT scores that were 140 points higher than Hispanics and 240 points higher than blacks.

To force the issue on a legal level, a freshman at Yale filed a complaint in the fall with the Department of Education's Office of Civil Rights, contending he was denied admission to Princeton because he is Asian. The student, Jian Li, the son of Chinese immigrants in Livingston, N.J., had a perfect SAT score and near-perfect grades, including numerous Advanced Placement courses.

"This is just a very, very egregious system," Mr. Li told me. "Asians are held to different standards simply because of their race."

Discrimination Against Asians

To back his claim, he cites a 2005 study by Thomas J. Espenshade and Chang Y. Chung, both of Princeton, which concludes that if elite universities were to disregard race, Asians would fill nearly four of five spots that now go to blacks or Hispanics. Affirmative action has a neutral effect on the number of whites admitted, Mr. Li is arguing, but it raises the bar for Asians. The way Princeton selects its entering class, Mr. Li wrote in his complaint, "seems to be a calculated move by a historically white institution to protect its racial identity while at the same time maintaining a facade of progressivism."

Private institutions can commit to affirmative action, even with state bans, but federal money could be revoked if they are found to be discriminating. Mr. Li is seeking suspension of federal financial assistance to Princeton. "I'm not seeking anything personally," he says. "I'm happy at Yale. But I grew up thinking that in America race should not matter."

Admissions officials have long denied that they apply quotas. Nonetheless, race is important "to ensure a diverse student body," says Cass Cliatt, a Princeton spokeswoman. But, she adds, "Looking at the merits of race is not the same as the opposite"—discrimination.

Elite colleges like Princeton review the "total package," in her words, looking at special talents, extracurricular interests and socioeconomics—factors like whether the applicant is the first in the family to go to college or was raised by a single mother. "There's no set formula or standard for how we evaluate students," she says. High grades and test scores would seem to be merely a baseline. "We turned away approximately half of applicants with maximum scores on the SAT, all three sections," Ms. Cliatt says of the class Mr. Li would have joined.

In the last two months, the nation has seen a number of new challenges to racial engineering in schools. In November, the United States Supreme Court heard a case questioning the legality of using race in assigning students to public schools in Seattle and Louisville, Ky. Voters are also sending a message, having thrown out racial preferences in Michigan in November, following a lead taken by California, Texas, Florida and Washington. [In December 2006] Ward Connerly, the architect of Proposition 209, announced his next potential targets for a ballot initiative, including Arizona, Colorado, Missouri and Nebraska.

When I ask the chancellor at Berkeley, Robert J. Birgeneau, if there is a perfect demographic recipe on this campus that likes to think of itself as the world's finest public university—Harvard on the Hill—he demurs.

"We are a meritocracy," he says. And—by law, he adds—the campus is supposed to be that way. If Asians made up, say, 70 percent of the campus, he insists, there would still be no attempt to reduce their numbers.

Asian enrollment at his campus actually began to ramp up well before affirmative action was banned.

Historically, Asians have faced discrimination, with exclusion laws in the 1800s that kept them from voting, owning property or legally immigrating. Many were run out of West Coast towns by mobs. But by the 1970s and '80s, with a change in immigration laws, a surge in Asian arrivals began to change the complexion of California, and it was soon reflected in an overrepresentation at its top universities.

In the late 1980s, administrators appeared to be limiting Asian-American admissions, prompting a federal investigation. The result was an apology by the chancellor at the time, and a vow that there would be no cap on Asian enrollment.

University administrators and teachers use anguished words to describe what has happened since.

"I've heard from Latinos and blacks that Asians should not be considered a minority at all," says Elaine Kim, a professor of Asian-American studies at Berkeley. "What happened after they got rid of affirmative action has been a disaster—for blacks and Latinos. And for Asians it's been a disaster because some people think the campus has become all-Asian."

Low Proportions of Blacks and Hispanics

The diminishing number of African-Americans on campus is a consistent topic of discussion among black students. Some say they feel isolated, without a sense of community. "You really do feel like you stand out," says Armilla Staley, a second-year law student. In her freshman year, she was one of only nine African-Americans in a class of 265. "I'm almost always the only black person in my class," says Ms. Staley, who favors a return to some form of affirmative action.

"Quite frankly, when you walk around campus, it's overwhelmingly Asian," she says. "I don't feel any tension between Asians and blacks, but I don't really identify with the Asian community as a minority either."

Walter Robinson, the director of undergraduate admissions, who is African-American, has the same impression. "The problem is that because we're so few, we get absorbed among the masses," he says.

Chancellor Birgeneau says he finds the low proportion of blacks and Hispanics appalling, and two years into his tenure, he has not found a remedy. To broaden the pool, the U.C. [University of California] system promises to admit the top 4 percent at each high school in the state and uses "comprehensive review"—considering an applicant's less quantifiable attributes. But the net results for a campus like Berkeley are disappointing. His university, Dr. Birgeneau says, loses talented black applicants to private universities like Stanford, where African-American enrollment was 10 percent last year—nearly three times that at Berkeley.

"I just don't believe that in a state with three million African-Americans there is not a single engineering student for the state's premier public university," says the chancellor, who has called for reinstating racial preferences.

One leading critic of bringing affirmative action back to Berkeley is David A. Hollinger, chairman of its history department and author of *Post-Ethnic America: Beyond Multiculturalism*. He supported racial preferences before Proposition 209, but is no longer so sure. "You could argue that the campus is more diverse now," because Asians comprise so many different cultures, says Dr. Hollinger. A little more than half of Asian freshmen at Berkeley are Chinese, the largest group, followed by Koreans, East-Indian/Pakistani, Filipino and Japanese.

He believes that Latinos are underrepresented because many come from poor agrarian families with little access to the good schools that could prepare them for the rigors of

Berkeley. He points out that, on the other hand, many of the Korean students on campus are sons and daughters of parents with college degrees. In any event, he says, it is not the university's job to fix the problems that California's public schools produce.

The Problem with Color Blind Admissions

Dr. Birgeneau agrees on at least one point: "I think we're now at the point where the category of Asian is not very useful. Koreans are different from people from Sri Lanka and they're different than Japanese. And many Chinese-Americans are a lot like Caucasians in some of their values and areas of interest."

If Berkeley is now a pure meritocracy, what does that say about the future of great American universities in the post-affirmative action age? Are we headed toward a day when all elite colleges will look something like Berkeley: relatively wealthy whites (about 60 percent of white freshmen's families make $100,000 or more) and a large Asian plurality and everyone else underrepresented? Is that the inevitable result of color-blind admissions?

Eric Liu, author of *The Accidental Asian: Notes of a Native Speaker* and a domestic policy adviser to former President Bill Clinton, is troubled by the assertion that the high Asian makeup of elite campuses reflects a post-racial age where merit prevails.

"I really challenge this idea of a pure meritocracy," says Mr. Liu, who runs mentoring programs that grew out of his book *Guiding Lights: How to Mentor and Find Life's Purpose.* Until all students—from rural outposts to impoverished urban settings—are given equal access to the Advanced Placement classes that have proved to be a ticket to the best colleges, then the idea of pure meritocracy is bunk, he says. "They're measuring in a fair way the results of an unfair system."

He also says Asian-Americans are tired of having to live up to—or defend—"that tired old warhorse of the model minority."

"We shouldn't be calling these studying habits that help so many kids get into good schools 'Asian values,'" says Mr. Liu, himself a product of Yale College and Harvard Law School. "These are values that used to be called Jewish values or Anglo-Saxon work-ethic values. The bottom line message from the family is the same: work hard, defer gratification, share sacrifice and focus on the big goal."

Different Approaches to Education

Hazel R. Markus lectures on this very subject as a professor of psychology at Stanford and co-director of its Research Institute for Comparative Studies in Race and Ethnicity. Her studies have found that Asian students do approach academics differently. Whether educated in the United States or abroad, she says, they see professors as authority figures to be listened to, not challenged in the back-and-forth Socratic tradition. "You hear some teachers say that the Asian kids get great grades but just sit there and don't participate," she says. "Talking and thinking are not the same thing. Being a student to some Asians means that it's not your place to question, and that flapping your gums all day is not the best thing."

One study at the institute looked at Asian-American students in lab courses, and found they did better solving problems alone and without conversations with other students. "This can make for some big problems," she says, like misunderstandings between classmates. "But people are afraid to talk about these differences. And one of the fantastic opportunities of going to a Stanford or Berkeley is to learn something about other cultures, so we should be talking about it."

As for the rise in Asian enrollment, the reason "isn't a mystery," Dr. Markus says. "This needs to come out and we shouldn't hide it," she says. "In Asian families, the No. 1 job of a child is to be a student. Being educated—that's the most honorable thing you can do."

Dispelling Stereotypes

Berkeley is "Asian heaven," as one student puts it. "When I went back East my Asian friends were like, 'Wow, you go to Berkeley—that must be great,'" says Tera Nakata, who just graduated and now works in the residence halls.

You need only go to colleges in, say, the Midwest to appreciate the Asian feel of this campus. But Berkeley is freighted with the baggage of stereotypes—that it is boring socially, full of science nerds, a hard place to make friends.

"About half the students at this school spend their entire career in the library," one person wrote in a posting on vault-.com, a popular job and college search Web site.

Another wrote: "Everyone who is white joins the Greek system and everyone who isn't joins a 'theme house' or is a member of a club related to race."

There is some truth to the image, students acknowledge, but it does not do justice to the bigger experience at Berkeley. "You have the ability to stay with people who are like you and not get out of your comfort zone," says Ms. Nakata. "But I learned a lot by mixing it up. I lived in a dorm with a lot of different races, and we would have these deep conversations all the time about race and our feelings of where we belong and where we came from." But she also says that the "celebrate diversity aspect" of Berkeley doesn't go deep. "We want to respect everyone's differences, but we don't mix socially."

Near the end of my stay at Berkeley I met a senior, Jonathan Lee, the son of a Taiwanese father and a mother from Hong Kong. He grew up well east of Los Angeles, in the New America sprawl of fast-growing Riverside County, where his father owned a restaurant. He went to a high school where he was a minority.

"When I was in high school," he says, "there was this notion that you're Chinese, you must be really good in math." But now Mr. Lee is likely to become a schoolteacher, much to the chagrin of his parents, "who don't think it will be very lucrative."

The story of Jon Lee's journey at Berkeley is compelling. As president of the Asian-American Association, he has tried to dispel stereotypes of "the Dragon Lady seductress or the idea that everybody plays the piano." His closest friends are in the club. It may seem that he has become more insular, that he has found his tribe. But Mr. Lee says he has been trying to lead other Asian students out of the university bubble. Once a week, they go into a mostly black and Hispanic middle school in the Bay Area to mentor students.

For the last five semesters, Mr. Lee has worked with one student. "I take him out for dim sum, or to Chinatown, or just talk about college and what it's like at Cal," he says. "We talk about race and we talk about everything. And he's taught me a lot."

The mentoring program came about not because of prodding by well-meaning advisers, teachers or student groups. It came about because Mr. Lee looked around at the new America and found that it looked very different from Berkeley. And much as he loves Berkeley, he knew that if he wanted to learn enough to teach, he needed to get off campus.

Analyzing White Studies
Courses in College Classrooms

The Journal of Blacks in Higher Education

The Journal of Blacks in Higher Education *is a monthly academic journal that examines the progress of African Americans in the nation's colleges and universities. In the following essay the journal's authors describe the newly emerging area of "whiteness studies" at U.S. universities. They examine the controversy surrounding this new field of study, including complaints by conservatives that while other ethnic studies programs celebrate the achievements and culture of that group, this new field focuses on how whites assumed the dominant position they now hold in American society, effectively demonizing the race.*

Since the onset of black studies programs in the late 1960s, a host of other ethnic studies programs have emerged on college campuses across the nation. Most common are programs in Chicano or Latino studies, Asian studies, Native American studies, women's studies, and gay and lesbian studies.

Now the concept of white studies or whiteness studies is beginning to take hold on college campuses. But unlike other ethnic studies programs, white studies is not a celebration of the history and culture of white Europeans and their American descendants. Rather, whiteness studies is an explicitly political field that examines how people of European descent developed the concept of race in order to enforce subordinate status on minority groups. For example, a Caucasian student who took a white studies course at the University of Massachusetts told the *Chicago Tribune*, "This was the first class that

The *Journal of Blacks in Higher Education*, "The Emergence of Whiteness Studies on America's College Campuses," winter 2003–2004, pp. 60–61. Reproduced by permission.

implicated me and showed me how I contributed to the system of oppression. It taught me that while people are racist, I'm racist, and the best way to dismantle it is to educate other white people so that antiracist whites are no longer in the minority."

In order to dispel beliefs that whiteness studies is a racist attack on Caucasians, a great majority of the white studies courses are taught by white faculty members.

Studying Institutional Racism

In the syllabus to his course Deconstructing Whiteness, Gregory Jay, a white professor of English at the University of Wisconsin, states that he taught the course because "white people need to take responsibility for race, since they invented the idea in the first place. Studying whiteness means studying institutional racism, especially practices that create white privilege. Silence about whiteness lets everyone continue to harbor prejudices and misconceptions, beginning with the notion that white equals normal. Whiteness oppresses when it operates as the invisible regime of normality. Whiteness is a way of distributing wealth and power according to arbitrary notions of biological difference."

Other courses are more philosophical rather than political in nature. Edwards Professor of American History Nell Irvin Painter of Princeton University taught a course several years ago called Whiteness in Historical Perspective. "It's revolutionary to make whiteness visible as a racial designation," Painter told the *Princeton Weekly Bulletin*. "Usually whiteness is unmarked, neutral. Part of being white is the privilege of not seeing yourself as marked. You do not spend your life being aware of your whiteness, unless you choose to do so."

Critics of whiteness studies see the field simply as an attack on the foundations of European-based white society. Conservative commentator David Horowitz summed up the critics' view: "Black studies celebrates blackness, Chicano studies celebrates Chicanos. Women's studies celebrates women and white studies attacks white people as evil."

Mathew Spaulding, the director of the Center for American Studies at the Heritage Foundation, told *The Washington Post* that whiteness studies is simply "a derogatory name for Western Civilization" and a vehicle for leftists who think that "black studies has not gone far enough in removing the baggage of Anglo-European traditions."

Conservative and often explicitly racist syndicated columnist Samuel Francis is even more blunt. He wrote: "The people who peddle whiteness studies make no pretense about their real purpose: to change how whites think about race so as to make whites feel guilt about who they are and what they or their ancestors have achieved, and thereby to destroy whites' capacity to resist being shoved aside by nonwhites."

White Studies Courses on Today's College Campuses

JBHE [*Journal of Blacks in Higher Education*] has conducted an extensive search of the curricula of the nation's leading colleges and universities to determine what, if any, courses on whiteness studies are being offered on these campuses. Here is a sampling of what we found:

- At Brown University there is a course entitled Critical Perspectives on whiteness. The course description says that it "investigates the cultural construction of race through an exploration of whiteness. How has whiteness been defined in relation to notions of color and race? What is 'white' identity? How is whiteness understood from a non-white perspective?"

- The English department at Swarthmore College offers the course Whiteness and Racial Difference. Classroom discussion counts for 25 percent of a student's grade. Students are also required to write two three-page papers and one 12-page research paper. There are no tests. Required reading for the course include Bell Hooks' *Ending Racism*, Ian F. Haney-Lopez's *White by Law*, and Robert Gossett's *Race: A History of an Idea in America.*

- The department of cultural and social anthropology at Stanford University offers Critical Perspectives on Whiteness. The course catalog offers this description: "After situating the construction of whiteness as an ethnic identity and social status in the first part of the course, we will examine collective and individual notions of this identification as it is co-constructed with notions of race, ethnicity, class, gender, sexuality, and nation. By looking at how white identities are reproduced, maintained, and challenged in social relations, pop culture, the media, and current affairs, this course is aimed at examining how the idea of whiteness has come to be imbedded within cultural and material politics over time and space."

- The department of Scandinavian studies at the University of California at Berkeley offers the course Hyperwhite and the Color Line: Representations of Whiteness and Color in American Cultures. This course examines negative aspects of whiteness such as perceived sexual and emotional frigidity, nerdishness, lack of rhythm, and the propensity for social pathology such as serial killings. The professor's thesis is that "in order to preserve an unmarked and thus dominant status in society, whites have had to invent the category of hyperwhite, assigning the negative characteristics associated with whiteness to some subgroups of European American culture. Scandinavian Americans have occasionally occupied the hyperwhite position."

- At Oberlin College, the history department offers Unbearable Whiteness: Social Construction of a Racial Category. This upper-level class meets in the evening for two hours only once a week. Class participation counts for a major portion of a student's grade. The course description leads off with the statement, "People deemed to be white have accrued social, legal, and economic privileges at the expense of others deemed nonwhite. Hence the importance of whiteness as a racial category cannot be overestimated. This course examines the emergence of whiteness as a socially constructed racial identity. By critically focusing on whiteness, it explores the plasticity/rigidity of racial categories and the articulation of skin color with power."

CHAPTER 4

Race and Ethnicity
in the Arts and Media

Reinforcing Colonialist Concepts of Indigenous Peoples

Earl Shorris

Earl Shorris is a journalist, social critic, lecturer, and novelist who has written extensively on Mesoamerican literature. In the following review of Mel Gibson's film Apocalypto, *Shorris argues that the filmmaker exploits Maya culture and perpetuates racist stereotypes. Not only does Gibson misrepresent the Maya civilization of the past, says Norris, but with his film he has damaged what has painstakingly been built by indigenous peoples in recent years, misappropriating and doing violence to their culture.*

On the Yucatán peninsula, where many of the Maya of Mexico live, there is an often-told story about people like Mel Gibson, whose bloody movie in the Yucatecan Maya language, *Apocalypto*, will be released December 8 [2006]. I first heard the story from Miguel Angel May May, a tall man among the Maya, handsome, now in his 40s, with a touch of gray in his hair. He speaks Yucatecan Maya so eloquently that when young people who have begun to lose their language and culture first hear him, they shed tears for what has been and what can be in the Yucatán.

May May tells the story with the kind of rage and pride that Gibson tried to portray with his Scottish heroes in *Braveheart* and postapocalyptic picaros in *Mad Max*: "A Maya, of the middle class, like me," May May said, "went into a Ford dealership here in Mérida. He intended to buy a new pickup truck. He was well dressed, but clearly Maya. The dealer offered him ten pesos to wash a truck." It is a common experience for people of color in a white world. The Yucatán is not entirely a white world, yet the Maya suffer the most severe prejudice of any large ethnic group in Mexico. In the language of prejudice in Mexico, the Maya are said to be people with big heads and no brains, too short, too dark and with a strange, laughable Spanish accent. Gibson accepted the stereotype and embellished it.

To grasp what a racist act Gibson has committed in the making of his new film, it is necessary to understand the world of the Maya as it exists today. Perhaps realizing what has been done to the Maya in the film, Gibson has been seeking allies among Latinos and American Indians. He even went so far as to tell *Time* magazine, "The fear mongering we depict in this film reminds me a little of President [George W.] Bush and his guys."

Undoing the Work to Build Maya Autonomy

In fact, Gibson stepped into a delicate cultural situation and may have shattered much of what has been built by indigenous people, historians and linguists in recent years. Ethnic prejudice is as harsh in the Yucatán as anywhere in the Americas. I have seen it played out in the Maya villages as well as in the cities and on the beaches. When the Clemente Course, which educates indigenous people as well as the poor in seven countries, taught its first class in the Maya language and humanities in the small village of San Antonio Sihó, the students told me that when they took the bus to Mérida (a journey of more than fifty miles) they were afraid to speak Maya, because people would think them stupid Indians (Mayeros). After two years of study, José Chim Kú, the student leader of the class, said, "Now, when I ride on the bus, I speak only Maya." It took two years for the faculty, including May May, to effect the change, for the Maya have internalized their recent history. And like all people who live in the violent mirror of racial and ethnic hatred, they suffer for their suffering. It is the bitterest irony of colonialism.

In the film *Apocalypto*, which Gibson claims will make the Maya language "cool again," there are many major roles. The lead is a lithe, handsome young man, a dancer from Oklahoma named Rudy Youngblood. He has indigenous ancestors, but he is not Maya, and like most of the other featured players he is not a professional actor. None of the four other major parts went to Maya either. According to Gibson, they are played by people from the United States, and the other featured players are either from Mexico City or Oaxaca. Yet every word spoken in the film is in Yucatecan Maya, a difficult language to learn or even to mimic, because it is both tonal and accented.

It is not as if Gibson had few Mayeros to choose from. There are more than a million Maya in Mexico, and more than 100,000 of them are monolingual Yucatecan Maya speakers. Yet Gibson chose not one Maya for a featured role. In so doing, he has made a film that reinforces the prejudice against the Maya, who have defended their cultural autonomy as fiercely as any people on earth. Twice they repulsed the Spaniard Francisco de Montejo, before he occupied part of the peninsula in 1527. They continued to fight pitched battles against European cultural and political dominance until the end of the Caste War in the early twentieth century. And even now militant organizations deep in the jungles of the state of Quintana Roo practice ancient rituals and resist Occidental cultural and political hegemony, including the Gregorian calendar. But the people have never been attacked by Hollywood.

Like the owners of the resort hotels that line the beautiful beaches of Cancún and Cozumel, Mel Gibson cast no Maya to work on his project, except in the most minor roles. Maya nationalists think the hotels and tourist packages that use the word "Maya" or "Mayaland" (a translation of Mayab) should pay for what they appropriate for their own use. The Maya patrimony, they say, is neither gold nor silver nor vast stretches of rich farmland; they have only their history, their culture, themselves. Like the hotel owners who bring strangers to the Yucatán to do everything but labor in the laundries and maintain the grounds, Gibson has brought in strangers to take the good parts from the Maya. He said in an interview that he chose people who "looked like you imagined they should," but I have seen photographs of Rudy Youngblood, and he does not look like any Maya I ever saw. One can only ascribe the choice of Youngblood and the other non-Maya to stereotypes that Gibson has adopted.

Reinforcing Maya Stereotypes

In casting and producing the film Gibson reinforced a colonialist concept of indigenous people that has long existed in Mexico. Ancient Maya culture was extraordinary, as the rest of the world now recognizes. The Maya invented one of the few original systems of phonetic writing (we are familiar with the Chinese system and the one that culminated in Latin script). They worked with the concept of zero long before it was known in Europe. They were superb astronomers. Their art and architecture are now known and studied throughout the world. It is also true that they were warriors and that they engaged in human sacrifice, although not on the grand scale of the Mexica. Their ability to manage large-scale military and civic works was impressive. Maya literature has a long and grand history, from the ancient words incised in stone through the Pop Wuj (Popol Vuh) and the postinvasion books of Chilam Balam to the eighteenth-century poems ("Kay Nicte"—Flower Song—and others) to contemporary works, including brilliant poetry by Briceida Cuevas Cob in Yucatecan Maya and Humberto Ak'abal in Ki'che and Miguel Angel May May's delightful fables.

Culture doesn't sell tickets. Violence does. Gibson has made what he calls "a chase movie." As we saw his Scot disemboweled and his Jesus battered into bloody meat, we will now see a young Maya running through the jungle to escape having his still beating heart torn from his chest. The social philosophy of Jesus found no place in Gibson's *Passion of the Christ*, and the glory of Maya culture cannot be featured in a "chase movie." "Blood! More blood!" Gibson shouted during the filming.

According to the Maya calendar, the world will end in 2012, but there have already been four creations in the Maya vision of the cosmos, and there is no reason to think they do not expect another. For the title of his movie Gibson chose a Greek word related to the ideas in the Book of Revelation: apocalypse. Gibson has tried to sell the movie as an allegory, using the fall of Maya civilization to limn the war in Iraq. But it is not about Iraq, and the end of the Maya classic period took place many centuries before the period Gibson chose for his film. The only profound meaning one can take away from the film is that there is an intimate connection between racism and violence. The message of the production is that the Maya are unacceptable people; we do not want to look at them as they are now, and we despise them for what they were then.

A Latino Makes Shakespeare His Own

Antonio Ocampo-Guzman

Antonio Ocampo-Guzman is an actor, director, and teacher from Bogotá, Colombia, who heads master of fine arts performance for the School of Theatre and Film at Arizona State University. In the following essay, he adds his personal perspective on the discourse on colorblind casting in the United States. He recounts his experiences and training as a Shakespeare player and shows how Shakespeare has been fundamental to his artistic and personal growth. He also examines the use of Shakespeare in multicultural theater projects and asks if he has been deluding himself about Shakespeare's "universality."

The first time I played with Shakespeare was in my high school English class. I went to the Anglo-Colombian School in Bogotá, a private school sponsored in part by the British Council. Most of my teachers were adventurous young English women and men who loved teaching and traveling. My ninth-grade teacher, Mr. Brown, loved three other things: [William] Shakespeare, Monty Python, and beer. I was irrevocably infected. In Mr. Brown's class, I played Friar Lawrence in the "Romeo, Romeo, come forth, come forth thou fearful man" scene. Amazingly, my first experience with Shakespeare was also my first experience as a bilingual performer. I seem to remember being more interested in my costume—my father's bathrobe was passing as the Franciscan monk's habit—than in the words I was speaking. I remember it being lots of fun. I also remember that I was very good at it, even if English was not my first language.

Antonio Ocampo-Guzman, *Colorblind Shakespeare: New Perspectives on Race and Performance*. Danvers, MA: Routledge, 2006. Copyright © 2006 by Taylor & Francis Group, LLC. Republished with permission of Routledge, Taylor & Francis Group, conveyed through Copyright Clearance Center, Inc.

During my senior year, I was cast as Henry Irving in Christopher Durang's *An Actor's Nightmare,* and I had to deliver Horatio's "Two nights together have these two gentlemen" speech. That was my first experience in being coached to speak Shakespeare. . . .

During the years of my acting training at the Teatro Libre School in Bogotá, I played several Shakespearean roles, including Puck, Petruchio, Iago, and Lady Macbeth. Those explorations were more about character and emotion than language, because it is nearly impossible for Shakespeare's words to operate on a similar level in any other language than English. Still, it was fertile ground for a young actor. To be able to tap into the darkness of greed, ambition, hatred, and fear to bring to life characters that were so huge in the history of theatre: it gave me a certain pride to think that I, a Colombian actor, could play Shakespeare.

One afternoon, for some fundraising event, I was asked to read two Shakespeare sonnets in both English and Spanish. Although I cannot remember the exact sonnets now, I do remember how attentive the audience was when I read them in English. They looked at me differently, as if the foreignness of the English words made them even more attentive to me. In Spanish they were listening to what I was saying, but in English they were attentive in a different manner. I also remember a different physical sensation when I read in English: I was actively seeking more understanding from my audience. In a sense, I cared more about them than about the sonnets. These memories have just come to me as I write this, and I wonder if that was the first time the idea of playing Shakespeare in both languages was planted in my brain.

Fast-forward a number of years; it is 1995, and I am about to go onstage at the Strand Theatre in Boston as Julius Caesar in Shakespeare & Company's New England Tour production. About 1,500 high school students fill the venerable house with buzzing energy. It is our biggest house so far on the tour, and my fellow players and I know that they will be a tough crowd. Most of them are inner-city kids, and many are Latino. At the beginning of each performance we give some historical information and then state our names and the characters we play. After each name, the crowd applauds politely. Jeff Plitt, a handsome actor from somewhere in New England who plays Mark Antony, gets a thunderous reception. When it is my turn, I go out, look out at the huge auditorium, and decide to show off not only my big, Linklater-trained voice but also my rich Colombian accent. I look for audience members who look particularly Latino, and I dart my introduction at them: "My name is Antonio Ocampo, I'm from Bogotá, Colombia, and I AM Julius Caesar." I am not nearly as good-looking as Jeff, but I brought the house down. There was something more than just plain actor's vanity in this: I realized that as a Latino actor, I had a great opportunity to show these high school students that playing Shakespeare was not reserved for white actors. I think they understood this point, and that is what caused them to erupt in thunderous applause.

I came to this country in 1993 to participate in the month-long Intensive Training Workshop at Shakespeare & Company in Lenox, Massachusetts. The experience changed my life, not only as an actor but also as a person. What is most amazing about the aesthetic and the training of Tina Packer's indomitable company is the first basic step: find yourself through what you are speaking. I was being trained to reveal who I was through the speaking of Shakespeare. The first days of these training workshops are spent in intense sessions called, appropriately, "Basics." Each participant selects a piece of text to which he or she has some kind of connection. I chose Shylock's "Hath not a Jew eyes" because I had witnessed Antony Sher's Shylock in London the year before and had been profoundly moved by the humor and the sorrow of his performance. I thought that since I shared some of Shylock's experience as an outsider and a foreigner, the speech could work well for me in the training studio. I was the first one up to work on it. I displayed what I had been taught before—character and emotion. I used everything at my disposal—my voice, my body, my imagination—to indicate that I was a Jewish father who carried a huge grudge and now sought vengeance. I used everything except the words and my experiences. After some intensive coaching, I acknowledged how I had been picked on, insulted, and generally discriminated against for being a Colombian. The rage, sorrow, and loneliness I carried within became available to me. When I was almost spent and completely vulnerable in my own experience, I was asked to speak the lines again. It was a mind-blowing experience. I was using words written four hundred years earlier, words in my second language, and yet they were so accurate in revealing my predicament to others. I have not been the same actor, or the same director, or the same teacher since that experience. Shakespeare became my own because my own personal and emotional growth came through his words.

After "Basics" I was cast as Macduff in the "my pretty chickens and their dam" scene to continue the training. All the conflicting feelings about the civil war in Colombia—my family members and acquaintances being hurt, my uncle being kidnapped, and my impotence to alter these events— became superb fuel for me. After the last presentation of the scene, I could not stop weeping out of sheer joy and pride. I would now call myself an actor because I now knew how to tap into these personal experiences. More important, Shakespeare played an integral part in this personal and intellectual growth. Shakespeare helped me uncover these emotions and gave me a vehicle to create compelling theatre from them. . . .

Bilingual Shakespeare

My most important and most complex Shakespearean experience to date came in April 2005, when I directed a bilingual production of *Romeo and Juliet* as part of Florida State

University's [FSU] School of Theatre 2004–2005 season. For years I had been wondering what would happen if I encountered Shakespeare in my two languages at the same time. Would my creativity operate in different ways? Would my understanding of the play deepen? Would my fragile sense of belonging deepen? I was fortunate to have the support of the administration, faculty, staff, and students at FSU in this enterprise, as well as several talented young bilingual actors. Above all, I had Frankie Alvarez, a Cuban-American senior in the Bachelor of Fine Arts track. Building on the assumption that the story of the lovers is universally known, I sought to investigate whether anything new would be illuminated in the story by playing it simultaneously in English and Spanish. . . .

Frankie grew up in Miami, where the two languages coexist openly in everyday life. Although he had easy access to Spanish sounds, he fell into the common trap of thinking in English (his primary language) and translating the thoughts into Spanish (his original language). Because of this, during rehearsals he was reciting his lines and not really generating thoughts and feelings in both languages, which of course was vital for the success of the production. The solution was pretty simple, really. I had to direct him in Spanish for the Spanish scenes and in English for the rest. Frankie and I began to communicate very precisely as we simultaneously thought in English and Spanish. He recently wrote to me that his largest challenge was thinking in "Spanish during the Spanish parts. It was hard to let myself do that, because for years I had only thought in English. The point that I finally stopped translating words into English in my head and started to really think in Spanish, was a major factor in the development of Romeo. That is when my body and energies became more open and much more playful." The process was exhilarating, and a great learning experience for both of us. We discovered a precision of thought in our communication because we were using two languages. The challenge of meeting Shakespeare in both our languages was making us better theatre artists.

Playing with Shakespeare has indeed been meaningful and enriching to me on several levels. As an actor and director, it gives me great pride that I can master him whom so many call the greatest playwright in history—he who is called "universal." Playing with Shakespeare, anchored in the Shakespeare & Company aesthetic, I learned how to be a more compelling actor, a better listener, and a better thinker. Shakespeare not only has demanded that I be more personally invested in my work but also has contributed to my emotional development. For a Latino actor, mastering Shakespeare is an additional source of self-esteem, because I am able to master a language that so many native English speakers find challenging. It has been extremely beneficial for me to succeed at the constructed standard of my adoptive culture. As a teacher, I have been able to create similar experiences for young actors, including others whose first language is not English, prompting a sense of self-esteem and artistic worthiness similar to that I have felt since my early years at Shakespeare & Company. Without a doubt, Shakespeare has been a significant part of my artistic and personal life.

The (Possible) Delusion

That is all very well, but am I being deluded? I am fully aware of how much Shakespeare has meant to me, but I am also aware how unexamined my experience has been to date. I must analyze why Shakespeare has been so unquestionably special to me personally. Why is he a landmark of my adopted culture? And how do I reconcile that fact with the current multicultural theatre practices that I support as a Latino artist?

On a very basic level, I recognize that yes, indeed, there are pieces of Shakespeare that are as phenomenal as [Ludwig von] Beethoven, [Pablo] Picasso, Martha Graham, and [Gabriel] García Márquez. There are elements of Shakespeare that rightly place him among the wonders of human creativity, and as such, I have as much right to enjoy and work with him as any other artist in the world. But I must also recognize that there is a lot of his work that is questionable. There are aspects of Shakespeare that are offensive to a twenty-first-century liberal sensibility: sexism, racism, xenophobia [fear of anything or anyone foreign], and homophobia. Some of it is very weak theatre, and many scenes simply do not work on stage today, which is why most of us who direct it end up cutting, adapting, updating, and manipulating it in order to have a compelling evening of theatre. In my respect and admiration, have I forgotten to illuminate those aspects of the Bard for myself as well as for my students? Have I been unknowingly manipulated by a social construct that I have not yet examined? Why, as a Colombian theatre artist, have I not challenged myself to work with any of the greatest playwrights in the Spanish-speaking canon? Why, as a Latino teacher, do I not challenge non-Anglo students to master the playwrights in their own languages?

My experiences at Shakespeare & Company were immensely eye-opening on many levels, certainly as an artist, discovering my deep intricacies and the tools to create compelling theatre with those raw materials. It also taught me about the cultural make-up of this country and the role that art plays in it. It brought to my attention two intriguing concepts I had never before encountered: arts in education and multiculturalism. . . .

There is something unparalleled in the way Shakespeare inquired about the world that makes it possible for us to do the same through his lens. I believe it stems from Shakespeare's language; his words are powerfully precise and intensely revealing. The rhetorical devices used to persuade, argue, and comprehend the world of [Shakespeare's characters] Hamlet, Lear, Romeo, Cleopatra, and Brutus are immensely beneficial to the education of young students. Shakespeare makes us more articulate, more able to name our experiences, and better equipped to shape the experiences of our lives. When so much of our culture turns superficially visual and disposable, it is imperative that we inculcate our youth with the love of knowledge and passion for learning, the clarity and precision of thought, and the need for inquiry in which Shakespeare, at his best, excels. Even writing these words now, I do not think I would have been able to comprehend and articulate all these complex thoughts if I had not struggled with [the roles of] Shylock, Macduff, Richard III, and others. They have helped me become a better thinker, listener, and speaker. In that respect, I am a champion for Shakespeare to be seminal in the education of our youth. For exactly the same reasons, I am a champion for Shakespeare to be seminal in the training of young actors, regardless of their heritage and ethnicity.

I have come to realize, however, that my championing of Shakespeare does have a limit. I have been very fortunate that in my training at Shakespeare & Company I was always allowed to sound Latino. No one ever suggested that my English was not good enough for Shakespeare. We did a great amount of voice training, based on Kristin Linklater's "Freeing the Natural Voice" approach, in which an actor's voice is freed from the limitations of habit and psycho-physiological disconnect. But we never engaged in the kind of speech and accent reduction that permeates much of actor training in this country. Even at the dawn of the twenty-first century, I have witnessed countless auditions and performances in which American actors of diverse ethnicities struggled through Shakespeare in a horrific semblance of "received pronunciation," as if they had been instructed that in order to do Shakespeare they must sound British. . . .

Regardless of linguistic history and background, it is imperative for an actor to achieve three main vocal objectives. An actor needs to be heard by the audience; an actor needs to be understood by the audience; and an audience must be able to follow an actor's train of thought. Voice training must be designed to help the actor achieve these goals with maximum efficiency. I contend that if the free and natural sounds of an actor are replaced to fit a constructed standard, the actor's psycho-physiological instrument is negatively affected. To tell someone that the way he or she sounds is not good enough, and specifically not good enough for Shakespeare, is oppressive. If Shakespeare is a paragon of human creativity, we all have a right to access him from our own identities. If Shakespeare holds the mirror up to nature, it ought to reflect our current cultural spectrum and the sounds and colors of our contemporary culture. These thoughts lead me to multicultural theatre and the notion of colorblind and "colordeaf" casting of Shakespeare.

Multicultural Theater

I assume that multicultural theatre is one where many cultures are represented by the theatrical experience, and not only onstage. I assume that multicultural theatre means theatre that tells stories from different cultural perspectives, from playwright to designer, director to performer, and audience to critic. If so, then the question that I must wrestle with next is: What is the purpose of having people of different cultural and linguistic backgrounds perform Shakespeare as a multicultural experience? What do I aim to illuminate by that practice? . . .

My production of *Romeo and Juliet* also did not really illuminate the play in new ways. We were very fortunate that our first preview audience was a group of high school students, bused in for the performance. Teenagers at a play do not lie: they do not suspend their disbelief easily, and they will not be polite if bored. For that reason, they are extremely dangerous and rewarding audiences. As they filled the theatre, I was very nervous, wondering how the bilingual experiment would work out. I could gauge that very few of the students were of Hispanic background, but I knew that several were studying Spanish, and I hoped that our experiment might be an added treat for them. The reception of the play by these high school students was overwhelming. They enjoyed the play immensely, and to my perception, were able to relate to the characters and the story in a surprising way. We got several comments such as "I never thought this could be so much fun." Yet, to my great disappointment, playing in two languages simultaneously was not the big deal I hoped it would be. It had an effect on how the students listened, but it really did not illuminate anything new in the story of the play. One young student told me that she was able to understand the "old" English better because from time to time she had to listen more intently to compensate for her lack of Spanish.

This reminds me of the afternoon when I recited the sonnets back in Bogotá. Maybe being bilingual allows us to be more efficient in our use of language, not only in the speaking of it but indeed, in the listening to it. And that is why I think these students were able to enjoy the play so much: they were really being "audiences," hearing the play, as Elizabethans would. "Let's go hear a play" was the phrase used by the Elizabethans, not our "Let's go see a play." Shakespeare wrote for an audience who participated fully in the performance, an audience eager to hear and enjoy language—words, reason, and rhetoric—through which the human predicament is illuminated. These high school students certainly were that: they played along with us as an important element, and the actors had a fantastic time because the audience was alive with them, responding to and returning energy. The bilingual experiment had a positive effect on the educational experience of these students, but I am not convinced that it helped illuminate the actual story or the relationships in new ways.

To my even greater disappointment, our predominantly adult and predominantly white audiences did not respond nearly as generously. Generally speaking, the adult audiences were very resistant to the untraditional delivery of the text and to the bilingual experiment. I had endeavored to make the language as visceral and powerful as possible, not a mere intellectual feast of beautiful sounds. There is a lot of sexuality in the play, and I had brought that to the foreground as well: our audiences did not seem to enjoy that. Possibly, they had a preconceived notion of what is "good and proper" Shakespeare, and my production did not match it in sounds, sights, or actions. We did not even have a balcony! And overall, they did not respond to the bilingual nature of the play; some even felt alienated by the Spanish. The worst possible comment I received was from one of the board members, who said to me that she thought the use of Spanish was "cute." With a broad smile, she said how much it served our "minority" students. Her words cut through me. "Cute" spoke of my experiment being superficial, and possibly even arrogant. It made me cringe that this board member infantilized my experiment, as if the exploration of the "sacred cow" by the ever-present Latino theatre artist was a necessary evil, but a silly one at best. Her words suggested that my attempt to make Shakespeare my own was not even worthy of attention; instead, she viewed it as a futile exercise and a misguided interpretation of the Bard of Avon. I learned that even in the theatre, even at an academic institution, there is linguistic as well as racial discrimination. I must accept that some in the audience were not open-minded enough to enjoy different languages. We had dared to toy around with one of the paragons of white, Anglo theatre, and they were not amused.

Maybe this sort of experiment would have worked better in a more urban setting than Tallahassee [Florida]. And yet, on a certain level, I am to blame for the experiment failing. I committed a huge mistake: I decided not to give any specific context to the bilingual nature of this world because I did not want to make a political statement, just an artistic one. Given the fact that the prevailing language of the play was English, there needed to be a significant political context to explain why one of the most powerful houses in this world used a different language. Without this clearly examined and defined context, playing *Romeo and Juliet* in both languages made no sense to the story of the play. Maybe it would have served the story better to have the linguistic and cultural differences between the two families be at the center of their brawl. Maybe it would have been a more compelling challenge for Prince Escalus to keep two disparate cultures from erupting into constant civil strife. Maybe it would have been more meaningful to have two young people from clearly defined different backgrounds fall in love to illuminate the transcendent nature of love, and to use the two languages to deepen their connection further. Overall, I believe this bilingual *Romeo and Juliet* was a positive educational experience, but not a very compelling artistic one because, just like the *Comedy of Errors* production, it remained unexamined.

I do not think I have been deluding myself. Instead, I think I have been wearing horse blinders which I must now remove. I do know I have mastered Shakespeare's theatre, but I need to examine its cultural politics much more deeply if I am going to find its true significance for me, my students, and my audiences. The cultural politics have to begin with the possibility of participation. Shakespeare's stories are very deeply anchored in worlds that are racist, homophobic, and xenophobic. Nontraditional casting is absurd unless the structure of the worlds represented in the plays is thoroughly examined and reinvented to contextualize colorblind and colordeaf casting choices. I must tackle Shakespeare in a new way, with more awareness of the cultural politics of performance and a deeper examination of my own participation in that performance—as a Latino artist living and creating within a culturally diverse society. Only then will I truly make Shakespeare my own.

When Race-Based Humor Fails

Marty Beckerman

Marty Beckerman determines that race-based humor is every-where, but it has different effects depending on its speaker and context. He argues that in the cases of Don Imus and other popular media and political personalities who have used race-based humor to entertain, they express themselves and direct their remarks toward a certain individual or group rather than illuminating the source of racial concerns and stereotypes within society. Meanwhile, many TV comedians and popular TV shows use race-based humor of the same kind, but audiences react differently since it appears as a critique of political correctness that can be shared with all people rather than an expression of personal opinion. Beckerman is the author of Generation S.L.U.T., *a commentary on teenage sex and culture.*

If the Easter decorations are still hanging around the Don Imus household, the craggy, cranky shock jock might feel inspired to study Jesus' discourse on judging others: This mulleted cracker-ass cracker has *no* business mocking *anyone's* hairstyle.

On Monday, the radio personality received a two-week suspension from NBC and CBS Radio for insulting the nappy-headedness of certain "hos" on the Rutgers basketball team. He appeared on Al Sharpton's radio show to apologize and explained that he was simply "trying to be funny" and "didn't think it was a racial insult," adding that "I can't get anywhere with you people." (A displeased Sharpton, echoing the angry midget's line from *Bad Santa* replied, "What do you mean by 'you people'?")

Previous Scandals

This scandal comes on the heels of *Seinfeld* star Michael Richards's race-baiting tirade last fall and right-wing author Ann Coulter's use of the word "faggot" at this year's CPAC [Conservative Political Action Conference] convention; in both cases the ugliest words in the English language were played for laughs and received contempt instead. (I would congratulate Coulter for landing the role of Skeletor in the inevitable remake of *Masters of the Universe*, but a Google search for "Ann Coulter, Skeletor" garners 12,800 hits; apparently I have my own problems with wit.)

All three instances of failed shock humors—Richards's, Coulter's and Imus's—led to condemnations and calls for sensitivity from a myriad of politicians and activists; Democratic Senator and Savior Barack Obama chastised Imus for his "divisive, hurtful and offensive" words, further suggesting that no one with "a public platform" should attempt to find humor in race-based stereotypes.

Popular Media's Race-Based Humor

The problem with this viewpoint is that the majority of Americans—of *all* colors and classes—have laughed at these hideous prejudices at some point; if you try to disassociate yourself from the hordes of hatemongers, your DVD collection better not include anything with Dave Chappelle, Chris Rock, Eddie Murphy, Sacha Baron Cohen, Mel Brooks, Trey Parker or Matt Stone. (If your DVD collection includes the abominable plagiarist Carlos Mencia, however, may God have mercy on your soul.)

From Lenny Bruce to *Reno 911!* American humor's most fertile ground has always been our racial, ethnic and religious dissimilarities, hypocrisies and insecurities; the P.C. [political correctness] witch hunts of the 1990s provided the fodder for numerous episodes of *Seinfeld* and *South Park*, which millions of Americans—most of whom would find real-life discrimination repulsive—enjoyed *because* they invoked "hurtful" stereo-types and provided a pressure release valve for our collective guilt, anger, confusion and repression. As any successful humorist will tell you, the most common praise comes in the form of "you say the things that everyone thinks but never admits!" Since most people can lose their jobs for tactless one-liners, the responsibility falls on our beloved entertainers.

On the other hand many bigots utilize shock humor as a means of clarifying and reinforcing group solidarity; spend a few minutes with certain cliques of College Republicans and you'll hear black babies compared to bowel movements and AIDS praised as God's cure for homosexuality. As one GOP [Grand Old Party, the acronym of the Republican party] devotee at American University told me, "You shouldn't go to jail for dragging gay people from your truck because it's not like they're human anyway." (Ha! Ha! Good one, old sport!) Senator Trent Lott and former Rep. John Cooksey, who defended the racial profiling of anyone who wears a "diaper on his head," have made similarly jaw-dropping gaffes in attempts at jest.

The Humor of Bigotry

So when does race-based humor qualify as harmless entertainment—albeit risqué and provocative—and when does it qualify as actual racism?

With my friends of other ethnic backgrounds—and okay, I probably need some more of these—the back-and-forth of boorish jokes is simply a way to kill time, share a few laughs and ease subconscious tension: the other night I joked that my Japanese immigrant friend should have applied for a yellow card instead of a green card; he fired back that if my bad Jewish self ever walked into a brick wall with an erection, I'd suffer a broken nose. (Neither of us felt the need to file a petition with the Anti-Defamation League, although I might need to watch my back for the little guy's razor-sharp throwing stars.) The wider American culture's embrace of stereotype-laced humor serves a similar purpose to our banter: *making people feel more comfortable with one another so they can get past their prejudices.*

This is why Richards, Coulter and Imus landed on their faces even though Americans *love* to laugh at bigotry: these entertainers poured salt into centuries-old wounds with cheap punch lines—simple, worthless slurs; spiteful, desperate pleas for attention—instead of throwing our collective ridiculousness back into our faces. Their sin had nothing to do with edgy jokes; it was that instead of shedding light on everyone, they only shed light on themselves.

CHAPTER 5

Reflections on Race and Ethnic Identity

A Korean-American Adoptee Embraces His Identity

Karen Fanning

At least 1.5 million adopted children are living in the United States today. Karen Fanning tells the life story of Keith Rutkowski, the adopted son of an American family, whose biological mother is still in Korea. He grew up fielding questions and teasing about his looks, but by the eighth grade he was active with a group devoted to educating people about adoption. After spending time in Korea, meeting his birth mother, and reflecting on his life, he now feels proud of his ethnic identity and all that contributes to it. Fanning writes for Scholastic News Online.

Keith Rutkowski is American. The 19-year-old college sophomore grew up in Canton, Massachusetts. He went on camping trips with his family, laughed and fought with his older sister, and competed as a sprinter and long jumper in track in high school.

Keith Rutkowski is Korean. He was born in Korea to a woman who was not married. She gave him up for adoption when he was an infant in order to give him a better life. He has never met his birth father. The Rutkowskis adopted Keith when he was 3 months old and raised him as their own. "My (adoptive) parents gave me all the values and morals I hold," Keith told Choices. "They supported me and gave me all the love and attention any child would want or need."

It was clear, though, that Keith's physical features were different from those of his adoptive Caucasian family. And he lived in the predominantly white town of Canton. Keith was the only Asian child in his elementary school.

Karen Fanning, "One Life, Two Countries: Raised by Loving Parents in the United States, This Teen Traveled Thousands of Miles to Complete His Family," *Scholastic Choices*, vol. 20, November–December 2004, pp. 6–12. Copyright © 2004 by Scholastic Inc. Reprinted by permission of Scholastic Inc.

"When I was younger, the only time I questioned how I looked was when kids asked me why I didn't look like my parents, or when I had to do a family tree," Keith says.

Things got tougher when Keith entered middle school. "Kids started teasing me about my eyes," he says. "They would ask me why I didn't look like my parents. I've always been open about my adoption, so I wasn't afraid to tell them I was adopted and was born in Korea. The teasing stopped when I stood up for myself."

Speaking Out

Keith also decided to speak out for others. In the eighth grade, he joined the Massachusetts Families for Kids Speak Out Team. The group of 125 teenagers travels to schools and conferences educating parents, teachers, students, government officials, and others about adoption.

One year later, Keith's travels would take him much farther. Accompanied by his family, he went to the country of his birth: South Korea. Keith, then 15, remembers vividly the emotions that swept over him when he got off the plane after a long 14-hour flight. He had an instant bond with the native Koreans he was seeing for the first time.

"I was shocked to see all these people who looked like me," he says. "I felt like I fit in for the first time and that I was part of the country."

Keith spent two weeks in Korea, enjoying the food, language, and culture of his native land. But the experience also left him confused once he returned home to the US.

Identity Crisis

"I didn't really know where I fit in," Keith says. "I wanted to fit in with the Korean side of me, but that was only my physical features. I wanted to fit in with the Caucasian side of me, but that was only my last name and my parents."

It is common for teens who were adopted to struggle with issues of identity, says Kim Stevens, co-director of Massachusetts Families for Kids.

"All teens go through identity issues," Stevens says. "That's an age when they're supposed to negotiate how to have an identity separate from Mom and Dad. Adoptive kids already have an identity separate from their family by virtue of their birth. Now they have to figure out who they are in addition to the family they've grown up in, and they also start asking questions about the family they never knew."

Keith received counseling to help him sort out his feelings, and his adoptive family supported him during this tough time as well. "Having their support helped me a lot," Keith says. "I could find out who I was because they cared about my feelings about being Korean and being adopted."

Meeting Mom

His exploration into the Korean side of his life sparked Keith's interest in finding this birth mother. He wondered what she looked like, how she was doing, and where she lived.

His search began at the adoption agency that handled his adoption years earlier. After months of making phone calls and writing letters, it ended with Keith back on a plane to South Korea accompanied once again by his adoptive family. He was 16.

"I was eager to meet my birth mother, but I was nervous, too," Keith says. "This was someone who gave birth to me, but I hadn't known my whole life. I didn't know what she looked like."

Then there was the issue of having his two mothers meet, but Keith says he was never worried about that. "I knew it was going to go well," he says. "My adoptive mother was eager to meet her. I knew from the Korean culture that my birth mother would be warm and welcoming to my adoptive mother because when she gave me up for adoption, she knew I was going to a loving family."

Keith met his birth mother in the summer of 2001. "We just looked at each other for an hour and couldn't stop crying," he says.

Many Questions

Once the tears stopped flowing, Keith's head swirled with questions. Why was he given up for adoption? Did he have brothers or sisters? What was his birth mother's life like now?

She told him she was unwed when she got pregnant and wanted a better life for him. She said Keith didn't have any siblings. And although she never married, she held a steady job and had a supportive family and many friends.

As she spoke, some of their similarities were easily recognizable. They shared the same cheekbones and jawline. Keith also learned where he got his sprinting talent from: His birth mother had been a runner too.

Before parting ways Keith and his mom exchanged phone numbers and e-mail addresses. And as soon as Keith returned to the U.S., he wrote to her. He holds no anger towards his birth mother for giving him up for adoption. "I am happy and proud to be who I am now, knowing that she gave me up because she loved me," Keith says.

A Diverse Life

When it came time to attend college, Keith knew he wanted to attend a diverse university. Currently in his second year of college, Keith is pleased with his choice: George Mason University in Fairfax, Virginia.

"My friends in college are Muslim, Asian, Hispanic, Caucasian, and African-American," he says. "I'm accepted by all races there. I feel like I can fit in there."

And Keith no longer struggles with where he fits in at home. He now has room in his heart for all the important people in his life. That includes his adoptive family and his birth mother, whom he has visited two more times and corresponds with regularly.

"I have so much support from my family," Keith says. "My adoptive mother and birth mother write to each other and send gifts. Their relationship is a loving one. Now, I fully know who I am and where I come from. I am a Korean-American with two families, and I am proud to be both."

Protecting Immigrants' Rights

Cecilia Muñoz

Cecilia Muñoz is vice president for policy of the National Council of La Raza. In the following essay, she points out that while the balance of congressional forces looks good for a comprehensive and fair immigration reform legislation, even advocates are divided over a sticking point—what to do with temporary workers. It is a challenge that must not be avoided, she says, and insists that the undocumented migrant stream must be replaced with a safe, legal, worker-friendly visa program.

It looks like this might finally be the year [2007] of fair and comprehensive immigration reform. The major obstacle to it last year, the highly negative Republican House leadership that produced the Sensenbrenner bill, has been removed and both the Senate and the House appear poised to finally launch the kind of debate on immigration that the country needs and deserves.

For immigrant rights advocates, this is a moment to get serious about passing the best possible bill, a "moment of truth" about its content.

Legalizing Undocumented Immigrants

There's widespread agreement among advocates on the need for a program that would legalize the maximum possible number of the 12 million undocumented immigrants currently living and working in the U.S. Other elements of the bill, like the elimination of family visa backlogs, aren't controversial. But there's real doubt on another central element of comprehensive immigration reform: the creation of a worker visa program for immigrant workers who might come in the future.

Cecilia Muñoz, "Temporary Workers Must Be Included," *New America Media*, January 18, 2007. Copyright © Pacific News Service. Reproduced by permission.

There's reason for the opposition to temporary worker programs. The American experience with it hasn't been a happy one for workers. Latinos, in particular, remember the notorious bracero program [a policy that allowed Mexicans to work in the Unites States, particularly seasonal agricultural workers], which has become synonymous with worker abuse. They rightly insist that we not repeat the grave mistakes of the past.

One way to respond to this history is to insist that there be no worker program in an immigration bill, or that it be as small as possible. While the logic of this position, based on the ugly history of worker programs, isn't unreasonable, its outcome is likely to be quite harmful.

Don't Repeat Past Mistakes

It's important not to repeat the mistakes of the Immigration Reform and Control Act of 1986 (IRCA), which produced a legalization program and a stricter enforcement regime without recognizing that workers would continue to come and be subject to worse conditions under energized and stricter enforcement.

That mistake created the conditions that we're living with now: a sizeable undocumented community, unprecedented levels of workplace injuries and a political climate so hostile that local governments across the country are willing to harass anyone who looks like an immigrant, in the name of immigration control.

Perhaps the most tragic consequences are the terrible human costs of workplace raids, which terrify communities and separate families, and the horrible death toll at the border, which exceeds one death per day every year.

If we pass a bill that does what IRCA did, combine a legalization program with stricter enforcement while failing to create a new, safe and legal path for new workers who might come in the future, we will have failed.

We will have failed because immigrant workers will continue to come, and too many will die in the Arizona desert. We will have failed because the continued migrant stream will signal to voters that immigration reform didn't work, and public support for stricter, more outrageous enforcement efforts, including the curtailment of civil and human rights, will grow.

Instead, we must face the challenge of creating a worker visa program that shows that we have learned from the ugly history of the bracero program. We made a good start in last year's Senate bill, which contained a program that allows workers to enter legally and safely, change jobs, complain against unscrupulous employers and petition for themselves to become U.S citizens if they choose to remain in the United States.

Strengthening Protections for Immigrants

Just as importantly, the program contained crucial wage protections for U.S. workers in industries where immigrants will be arriving, ensuring that immigrants' wages do not undercut those of the existing workforce. There's more that we can do to strengthen the protections for immigrant workers and their co-workers in the U.S., and we must use every opportunity in this debate to win these indispensable protections.

But we must not allow ourselves to believe that legalization for those who are here is enough. We have a responsibility to those who will continue to come, and to the American workers who worry about the security of their jobs.

We must replace the undocumented migrant stream with a safe, legal, worker-friendly visa program. It's essential to winning the battle over our broken immigration system, and to winning the larger war that this ugly debate has become.

Organizations to Contact

The editors have compiled the following list of organizations concerned with the issues presented in this book. The descriptions are derived from materials provided by the organizations. The list was compiled on the date of publication of the present volume; the information provided here may change. Be aware that many organizations take several weeks or longer to respond to inquiries, so allow as much time as possible.

Anti-Defamation League

823 United Nations Plaza, New York, NY   10017
(212) 490-2525 • fax: (212) 867-0779
Web site: www.adl.org

The Anti-Defamation League (ADL), founded in 1913, is the world's leading organization fighting anti-Semitism through programs and services that counteract prejudice, bigotry, and all forms of bias-motivated hatred. The ADL Materials Resource Center offers extensive materials on prejudice, discrimination, ethnicity, stereotyping, and scapegoating. It also offers other tools designed to help schools and communities teach and learn about diversity and enhance understanding of different groups. The ADL Education Division and its A World of Difference Institute offer prejudice-reduction training for schools, colleges and universities, the workplace, and the community.

The Arab American Institute

1600 K Street NW, Suite 601, Washington, DC   20006
(202) 429-9210 • Fax: (202) 429-9214
Web site: www.aaiusa.org

The Arab American Institute (AAI) represents the policy and community interests of Arab Americans throughout the United States and strives to promote Arab American participation in the U.S. electoral system. AAI focuses on two areas: campaigns and elections and policy formation and research. The institute strives to serve as a central resource to government officials, the media, political leaders and community groups and a variety of public policy issues that concern Arab Americans and U.S.-Arab relations.

Asian American Institute

4753 North Broadway, Suite 904, Chicago, IL   60640
(773) 271-0899 • fax: (773) 271-1982
Web site: www.asianamerican.net

The Asian American Institute seeks to empower the Asian Pacific American community through advocacy, research, education, and coalition building.

Center for Living Democracy

289 Fox Farm Road, Brattleboro, VT   05301
(802) 254-1234 • Fax: (802) 254-1227
Web site: www.livingdemocracy.org

The Center for Living Democracy (CLD) is a nonprofit organization that seeks to strengthen democracy by encouraging Americans to engage in solving society's toughest problems. CLD gathers and shares materials produced from direct experience in communities across the nation and presents seminars and workshops for organizations seeking to create more effective democratic cultures. In October 1997 CLD published *Bridging the Racial Divide: A Report on Interracial Dialogue in America*, the results of a year-long survey of interracial dialogues occurring in more than thirty states. CLD researchers interviewed more than sixty groups that use sustained, community-based dialogue across the racial divide.

Center for the Study of White American Culture

245 West Fourth Avenue, Roselle, NJ   07203
Phone: (908) 241-5439 • fax: (908) 245-4972
Web site: www.euroamerican.org

The Center for the Study of White American Culture supports cultural exploration and self-discovery among white Americans. It encourages a dialogue among all racial and cultural groups concerning the role of white American culture in the larger American society.

Educators for Social Responsibility

23 Garden Street, Cambridge, MA   02138
(800) 370-2515 • fax: (617) 864-5164
e-mail: esrmain@igc.apc.org
Web site: www.benjerry.com/esr

Educators for Social Responsibility's (ESR) primary mission is to help young people develop the convictions and skills to shape a safe, sustainable, and just world. ESR is a leading national center for staff development, school improvement, curricular resources, and support for schools, families, and children. ESR works with adults to advance teaching social responsibility as a core practice in the schooling and upbringing of children. ESR is recognized nationally for its leadership in conflict resolution, violence prevention, intergroup relations, and character education. The Resolving Conflict Creatively Program, an initiative of ESR, is one of the largest and longest-running programs in conflict resolution and intergroup relations in the country.

Green Circle Program

1300 Spruce Street, Philadelphia, PA   19107
(215) 893-8400 • fax: (215) 735-9718

The Green Circle Program, a national organization since 1957, promotes respect, understanding, and acceptance of ethnic and racial diversity through an intergroup education program that contributes to communication skills, self-esteem, and responsibility. Workshops are based on the premise that recognizing and using individual differences strengthens the whole. The program works with all age groups and with anyone interested in building skills for living effectively with human differences. Green Circle uses interactive strategies that are structured for elementary school-aged children and develops education programs, workshops, and conferences for others who wish to address the issue of living with human differences.

Hope in the Cities

1103 Sunset Avenue, Richmond, VA   23221
(804) 358-1764 • fax: (804) 358-1769
e-mail: Hopecities@aol.com

Hope in the Cities is an interracial, multifaith national network that seeks to encourage a process of healing through honest conversations on race, reconciliation, and responsibility. It focuses specifically on the acknowledgment and healing of racial history, the sustaining of dialogues involving people of all races and viewpoints, and the acceptance of personal responsibility for the process of change. Hope in the Cities assists communities in building diverse coalitions with people in business, government, media, education, and religious and community organizations.

National Association for the Advancement of Colored People

4805 Mount Hope Drive, Baltimore, MD   21215
Web site: www.naacp.org

Founded in 1909, the National Association for the Advancement of Colored People (NAACP) is one of the oldest and most influential civil rights groups in the United States. Throughout its existence it has worked primarily through the legal system on behalf of the rights of African Americans, but its goal is also to ensure the political, educational, social, and economic equality of rights of all persons and to eliminate racial hatred and racial discrimination. Since 1910, the NAACP has published the *Crisis*, a magazine dedicated to discussing critical issues confronting people of color, American society, and the world in addition to highlighting the historical and cultural achievements of diverse peoples. In essays, interviews, and in-depth reporting, writers explore past and present issues concerning race and its impact on educational, economic, political, social, moral, and ethical issues.

National Conference for Community and Justice
71 Fifth Avenue, Suite 1100, New York, NY   10003
(212) 206-0006 • fax: (212) 255-6177

The National Conference for Community and justice (NCCJ), founded as the National Conference of Christians and Jews in 1927, is a human relations organization dedicated to fighting bias, bigotry, and racism in America. NCCJ promotes understanding and respect among all races, religions, and cultures through advocacy, conflict resolution, and education.

National Congress of American Indians
1301 Connecticut Avenue NW, Washington, DC   20036
Web site: www.ncai.org

The National Congress of American Indians (NCAI) was founded in 1944 in response to termination and assimilation policies that the United States forced upon the tribal governments in contradiction of their treaty rights and status as sovereigns. The NCAI stressed the need for unity and cooperation among tribal governments for the protection of their rights. Since 1944 the NCAI has been working to inform the public and Congress on the governmental rights of American Indians and Alaska Natives.

National Council for La Raza
1126 Sixteenth Street NW, Washington, DC   20036
(202) 785-1670 • fax: (202) 776-1792
Web site: www.nclr.org

The National Council of La Raza (NCLR), the largest national Hispanic civil rights and advocacy organization in the United States, works to improve opportunities for Hispanic Americans. The NCLR conducts applied research, policy analysis, and advocacy, providing a Latino perspective in five key areas—assets/investments, civil rights/immigration, education, employment and economic status, and health. It produces research reports and more general publications on issues such as health care, poverty, immigration, civil rights, and education.

National MultiCultural Institute

3000 Connecticut Avenue NW, Suite 438
Washington, DC   20007
(202) 483-0700 • fax: (202) 483-5233
e-mail: nmci@nmci.org
Web site: www.nmci.org

The National MultiCultural Institute (NMCI) is a private, nonprofit organization founded in 1983 to promote understanding and respect among people of different racial, ethnic, and cultural backgrounds. NMCI provides a forum for discussing the critical issues of multiculturalism through biannual conferences, diversity training and consulting, special projects, resource materials, and a multilingual mental health referral network. NMCI provides training and technical assistance on all aspects of organizing and facilitating dialogue groups.

National Urban Leage

120 Wall Street, 8th Floor, New York, NY   10005
(212) 558-5300 • fax: (212) 344-5332
Web site: www.nul.org

The National Urban League is the nation's oldest and largest community-based movement devoted to empowering African Americans to enter the economic and social mainstream. Since its formation in 1910, the National Urban League has published books, magazines, and other publications, that capture, illustrate, and provide insight into the black experience in America. The league's publications include the annual report *The State of Black America* and *Opportunity Journal*, a quarterly magazine offering in-depth and scholarly analysis of the issues of the day. The league's Policy Institute, its think tank, produces a number of special reports throughout the year that examine the impact of economic social, and political issues on the black condition.

Project Change
Tides Center, San Francisco, CA   94129
(415) 561-6400

Project Change is a funding initiative aimed at helping communities reduce racial prejudice and improve race relations. Working closely with community-based coalitions in selected communities, Project Change seeks to develop locally driven strategies to reduce the incidence of racism as well as to dismantle the institutional structures that sustain its effects.

Study Circles Resource Center
697A Pomfret Street, Pomfret, CT   06258
(860) 928-2616 • fax: (860) 928-3713
e-mail: scrc@neca.com

The goal of the Study Circles Resource Center (SCRC) is to advance deliberative democracy and improve the quality of public life in the United States. SCRC helps communities use study circles—small, democratic, highly participatory discussions—to involve large numbers of citizens in public dialogue and problem solving on critical issues such as race, crime, education, youth issues, and American diversity. Through dialogue on matters of public concern, citizens gain ownership of issues and see themselves as people who can effect change at the local level. In the area of race relations, the SCRC works with community leaders at every stage of creating community-wide study circle programs helping organizers network between communities, working to develop strong coalitions within communities, and providing free discussion materials and comprehensive technical assistance.

YWCA of the U.S.A.
Office of Racial Justice and Human Rights
New York, NY   10116
(212) 273-7827 • fax: (212) 273-7849

The YWCA of the U.S.A. operates in more than 4,000 locations throughout the country in 400 associations in all 50 states. Its outreach extends internationally through its membership in the World YWCA, at work in more than 90 countries. For decades, the YWCA has pioneered efforts to eliminate racism through programs and advocacy. The organization's vision of empowering women through the elimination of racism and sexism remains its driving force. The Office of Racial Justice and Human Rights at the YWCA of the U.S.A. provides resources, training, and technical assistance to the local community and student YWCA associations to develop collaborative programs and strategies with other organizations to eliminate institutional racism at the local level in education, law enforcement, housing, health care, finance, and other institutions.

Bibliography

Books

Kwame Anthony Appiah — *The Ethics of Identity*. Princeton, NJ: Princeton University Press, 2005.

Eduardo Bonilla-Silva — *Racism Without Racists: Color-Blind Racism and the Persistence of Racial Inequality in the United States*, 2nd ed. New York: Rowman & Littlefield, 2006.

Alejandro del Carmen — *Racial Profiling in America*. New York: Prentice Hall, 2007.

Ashley W. Doane and Eduardo Bonilla-Silva, eds. — *White Out: The Continuing Significance of Racism*. New York: Routledge, 2003.

Michael Eric Dyson — *Come Hell or High Water: Hurricane Katrina and the Color of Disaster*. New York: Basic Civitas, 2006.

Michael Eric Dyson — *Debating Race*. New York: Basic Civitas, 2007.

Henry Louis Gates Jr. — *America Behind the Color Line: Dialogues with African Americans*. New York: Warner Books, 2004.

Henry Louis Gates Jr. — *Finding Oprah's Roots: Finding Your Own*. New York: Crown, 2007.

Andrew Garrod and Robert Kilkenny, eds. *Balancing Two Worlds: Asian American College Students Tell Their Life Stories*. Ithaca, NY: Cornell University Press, 2007.

Jorge J.E. Gracia *Race or Ethnicity?: On Black and Latino Identity*. Ithaca, NY: Cornell University Press, 2007.

Yvonne Yazbeck Haddad *Not Quite American?: The Shaping of Arab and Muslim Identity in the United States*. Waco, TX: Baylor University Press, 2004.

Yvonne Yazbeck Haddad, Jane I. Smith, and Kathleen M. Moore *Muslim Women in America: The Challenge of Islamic Identity Today*. New York: Oxford University Press, 2006.

Kofi Buenor Hadjor *The Changing Face of Race in America: The Role of Racial Politics in Shaping Modern America*. Trenton, NJ: Africa World Press, 2007.

Arar Han and John Hsu, eds. *Asian American X: An Intersection of Twenty-First-Century Asian American Voices*. Ann Arbor: University of Michigan Press, 2004.

Chester Hartman and Gregory D. Squires, eds. *There Is No Such Thing as a Natural Disaster: Race, Class, and Hurricane Katrina*. New York: Routledge, 2006.

Melanie Kaye-Kantrowitz *The Colors of Jews: Racial Politics and Radical Diasporism*. Bloomington: Indiana University Press, 2007.

Melanie   *The Hip Hop Generation: Young*
Kaye-Kantrowitz   *Blacks and the Crisis in African*
                  American Culture. New York: Basic
                  Civitas, 2002.

Bakari Kitwana   *Why White Kids Love Hip-Hop:*
                  Wankstas, Wiggers, Wannabes, and the
                  New Reality of Race in America. New
                  York: Basic Civitas, 2005.

Douglas Stuart   *We Were Taught to Plant Corn, Not to*
London and Tax'a *Kill: Secrets Behind the Silence of the*
Leon London   *Mayan People.* Guilford, CT: Back Up
                  Books, 2007.

Michelle Malkin   *In Defense of Internment: The Case*
                  for "Racial Profiling" in World War II
                  and the War on Terror. Washington,
                  DC: Regnery, 2004.

Roopali   *The Racial Order of Things: Cultural*
Mukherjee   *Imaginaries of the Post-Soul Era.* Min-
                  neapolis: University of Minnesota
                  Press, 2006.

Barack Obama   *Dreams from My Father: A Story of*
                  Race and Inheritance. New York:
                  Times Books, 1995.

Richard Perry   *"Race" and Racism: The Development*
                  of Modern Racism in America. New
                  York: Palgrave Macmillan, 2007.

Vincent Sarich   *Race: The Reality of Human Differ-*
and Frank Miele   *ences.* Boulder, CO: Westview, 2005.

Amartya Sen   *Identity and Violence: The Illusion of*
                  Destiny. New York: W.W. Norton,
                  2006.

Earl Shorris — *Latinos: A Biography of the People.* New York: W.W. Norton, 1992.

Audrey Smedley — *Race in North America: Origin and Evolution of a Worldview,* 3rd ed. Boulder, CO: Westview, 2007.

Juan Williams — *Enough: The Phony Leaders, Dead-End Movements, and Culture of Failure That Are Undermining Black America—and What We Can Do About It.* New York: Crown, 2006.

Joy M. Zarembka — *The Pigment of Your Imagination: Mixed Race in a Global Society.* Washington, DC: Madera, 2007.

Periodicals

Geneive Abdo — "America's Muslims Aren't as Assimilated as You Think," *Washington Post,* August 27, 2006, p. B3.

Karen W. Arenson — "At Princeton, a Parody Raises Questions of Bias," *New York Times* (January 23, 2007).

Ali S. Asani — "'So That You May Know One Another': A Muslim American Reflects on Pluralism and Islam," *Annals of the American Academy of Political and Social Science* 588 (July 2003): 40–51.

Allen C. Brownfeld — "American Jews Belong in Israel Declare Israeli Authors Yehoshua and Halkin," *Washington Report on Middle East Affairs,* August 2006, 54–55.

Stanley Feldman and Leonie Huddy — "Racial Resentment and White Opposition to Race-Conscious Programs: Principles or Prejudice?" *American Journal of Political Science* 49, no. 1. (January 2005): 168–183.

Renée A. Hill — "Seeing Clearly Without Being Blinded: Obstacles to Black Self-Examination," *Journal of Negro Education* 72, no. 2 (Spring 2003): 208–216.

Charles Hirschman — "The Origins and Demise of the Concept of Race," *Population and Development Review*, 30, no. 3 (September 2004): 385–415.

Journal of Blacks in Higher Education — "Can Hip-Hop Be the New Driving Force Behind Increased Racial Integration?" 38 (Winter 2002–2003): 64–67.

Journal of Blacks in Higher Education — "In Educational Attainment, Black Immigrants to the United States Outperform Native-Born White and Black Americans," 40 (Summer 2003): 51–52.

Kenneth Jost — "Understanding Islam," *CQ Researcher* 16, no. 39 (November 3, 2006): 914–936.

Bryan Monroe — "Beyond Imus, It's Time to Step Up: Disgraceful Episode Creates Opportunity to Reclaim Our Voice," *Ebony* 62, 8 (June 2007): 70.

Makani   "Co-opting Consumers of Color,"
Themba-Nixon   *Nation,* July 3, 2006.

Debby Thompson   "'Is Race a Trope?': Anna Deavere
                       Smith and the Question of Racial
                       Performativity," *African American
                       Review* 37, no. 1 (Spring 2003): 127–
                       138.

Cornel West   "Exiled from a City and from a Na-
                       tion," *Observer,* September 11, 2005.

Index